David, The Elder Apostle

The Story Of An Unknown Man Who Played A Key Role In The Life, Death and Resurrection Of Jesus Christ

Dr. J. David Lortscher

SHERRy - mAy THis Book Be A
Blessing TO you A-o To All oTHers
WHo REAo iT.

     W ArmesT RegARuS ...
       DR- DAve

Published by The Hallmark of Excellence, LLC
Moneta, Virginia

ISBN: 1-4752-4518-1
ISBN-13: 9781475245189

Dedication

This book is dedicated to Blessed Pope John Paul II, whose life of prayer, peace-making and writing inspired me to share this story as it was given to me by God

Introduction

"The music of this opera (Madame Butterfly) was dictated to me by God;

I was merely instrumental in putting it on paper and communicating it to the public."

Giacomo Puccini

At the end of your reading when you finish the last sentence of this book and lay it down, you may speculate about whether or not this story is true, whether or not it really happened, whether or not there was in fact an Elder Apostle named David.

Search the Old and New Testaments, and especially the Acts of the Apostles, and you will search in vain; there is no mention of such a person—not even a suggestion that such a person existed. Similarly, the rich oral traditions of the Christian Church (replete with hundreds of apocryphal stories of which a good many are likely to be true) make no mention of such an individual—none whatsoever.

Therefore, it's easy to dismiss this story as the mere imaginings of an over-active mind on the part of the author, until one learns that this story was given by a Source to the author all of a piece, complete and unvarnished, in living 3-D Technicolor, with the sights, sounds, smells, touches and even tastes of the experience vividly conveyed without editing or interpretation. Aspects of the story are beyond any author's imagining, which in a way make them more believable and real.

So, while the book categorizers may label this book "mere fiction," or "historical fiction" at best, I beg the reader to consider the following.

This story was given to me in digestible bites over a period of time. Each new bite complemented and enriched that which had already been conveyed. I saw people, places and events very, very clearly, and in fact, I had the sensation of "being there" myself. I began to believe that this story really happened, and furthermore, that for some unknown reason I had been chosen to tell it to the world. Consequently, in 2011 I traveled to the Holy Land and journeyed through Biblical Galilee, Judea and Palestine.

What I encountered was astonishing and also reassuring: the scenes firmly imprinted on my mind prior to my journey to Israel were accurate in every detail. Without ever having looked at a map of Israel, I already knew where everything was and how the landscape was patterned. I stood in many places that were exactly as I had "seen" them when given this story. In short, it was like I had already been there for a very long time, which I now believe to be the case. Otherwise, how could my knowledge be so breathtakingly real?

I believe God's intention in giving me this story and prompting me to write it for you is so that new dimensions of Jesus, his life, his followers and his ministry might be shared with legitimate seekers of a deeper understanding of redemption history and the role that one otherwise unknown man, David, the Elder Apostle, played in this salvation saga. It is my hope that the story enriches your faith and brings you closer to our Eternal God.

.

JACOB

My name is David, which in Hebrew means "the beloved one of God." My story begins with my father, Jacob. To say that my father profoundly affected my life is an understatement; he attempted to design, orchestrate and manage my life from my earliest years.

As an example, Jacob agreed to name me David, even though the Jewish tradition was to never name a child after the great King David because of the belief that no one would ever again match King David's greatness nor his contribution to the Jewish state. My father, however, was a member of the House of David and traced his lineage directly back to King David, and consequently he was actually pleased to make this fact known through the naming of his first-born son. Therefore, to the astonishment of the entire community and especially to the religious leaders, I was named David.

Jacob was one of the most powerful men in Jerusalem, with ready access to the highest levels of both Jewish and Roman authorities. He was a very successful and wealthy merchant, but he also had other widespread business interests as well. It seemed that everything he touched turned into riches for him and for our family.

Jacob was known as a ready dispenser of bags of coins. For instance, when a scandal surfaced among the Jews regarding Jacob's rumored commerce with the Romans, a few sacks of coins clandestinely slipped into the right pockets quickly silenced the critics.

My father was a short, slight man, but wherever he went and whomever he was with, he dominated the scene with his carriage and demeanor. He dressed richly but not in an overly ostentatious manner. He wore one gold pendant and one gold ring, but the gems in each were obviously of inestimable value. People clamored to be associated with him.

Jacob was a highly successful merchant, and his large shops displayed the finest cloth, herbs, tapestries, jewels, works of art, and other expensive merchandise from all over the world. His shops were a delight to the senses, with sights and smells of fine wine, olive oil, cheeses, foreign fruits and vegetables, and other esoteric imported items.

Our large shop was situated in a highly strategic location very near the Temple and also the Fortress of Antonio, which was the Roman headquarters. It was always Jacob's dream that I, as his first-born son, would succeed him in the business. From my earliest years, he brought me to the shop each day and instructed me in the ways of commerce.

However, I didn't like this life at all and had little aptitude for it. Bartering and haggling over prices was an established and even expected activity. When a purchase was about to be made, Jacob would indulge in telling the prospect that the cost was way below the value of the item, while the customer would loudly complain about being severely gouged by the exorbitant price Jacob quoted. Eventually a compromise price would be reached, with each party privately believing that he had gotten the better of the deal.

I was extremely sensitive and I dreaded these apparently heated exchanges, so I would retreat to the back storage room whenever a belligerent customer appeared. If forced to engage in such an exchange myself, I would rather quickly succumb to the customer's threats and give him the merchandise at a price below what I knew my father expected.

My younger brother, Aaron, was just the opposite. He readily grasped the intricacies of negotiating profitable sales, and he also understood other nuances of commerce far better than I. We eventually settled into an unspoken working arrangement whereby he usually interfaced with customers while I did the more menial, backroom chores such as sorting and stocking merchandise, cleaning, and other non-interpersonal tasks.

Over time, a not-so-subtle shift occurred. Whereas I used to accompany my father on buying expeditions to ports on the Mediterranean and other inland trade centers, I stopped being included and Aaron was invited to accompany my father instead. I was not overly troubled by this development, because I preferred to be alone anyway.

I feared my father and I knew that I didn't measure up to his expectations. However, I am especially grateful to him in one regard in particular. Aaron always wanted to be at the shop whenever possible, and so he only received the "mandatory" education experienced by most young Jewish boys. I, however, thrived on learning about moral and religious values and teachings, and my father made it a point to allow me to study extensively with the best Jewish rabbis and scholars of the time.

Whenever I had free time, I gravitated to the temple where I sat for long periods of time listening to the scholars discuss and debate religious scriptures and beliefs. I was content to sit in the background and listen for hours, and I had to reluctantly drag myself back to the shop when I was expected to resume work. Even in this regard, father was lenient about my comings and goings, and he seemed to sense that my future was somewhere else other than in commerce.

My father did what was expected of him as far as practicing the Jewish faith, but this was only a strategic move and not anything heartfelt on his part. He was not a religious man, but rather he was in fact caught up in a lifelong pursuit of more wealth and power. He contributed generously to the Temple authorities and secretly to the Romans, but all of his donations were well-conceived and always had a motive of personal gain attached.

I was surprised one day when he met me on the path leading from the temple to our shop, but not surprised by his words as we sat on a wall overlooking the Kidron Valley. He told me that it had become apparent that my heart wasn't in a life of commerce, and consequently he was bequeathing what should have been my first-born birthright to Aaron instead. He assured me that I would always be taken care of by him, and then by Aaron after his death, but that I would not have any part in the ownership of his estate. His pronouncement was factual and emotionless, and we walked back to the shop together. His primary reason for living was the attainment of more wealth and more power, and he had acted accordingly. I never knew he loved me until much later in my life.

BENJAMIN

One of the few visitors to the shop whom I was always eager to see was Benjamin, the leather-worker. He brought beautiful sandals, belts, girdles, pouches and other leather artifacts to sell to my father, who in turn marked them up exorbitantly and displayed them for sale. Benjamin was the only artisan with whom my father didn't haggle. My father always mercilessly argued down the prices asked for by silversmiths, goldsmiths, potters, weavers, and all manner of other craftspeople, but Benjamin was different. He asked for a fair price for his high-quality merchandise, and father paid it without a quarrel.

Benjamin was very quiet and unassuming, and I was drawn to him immediately. He was in his mid-forties and lived alone in a back room behind his small workshop, which was located at an intersection of two major streets in Jerusalem. Whenever he came into our shop, we would talk alone for a few minutes before he returned to his work. I cherished such times with Benjamin, especially since I had no other friends with whom to converse.

I sensed a deep inner worth and beauty in this humble artisan, and I realized later that a large part of my attraction to him was that he was a lot like me: unassuming, private, spiritual, and not caught up with temporal values of wealth, power, or pleasure. What I didn't know until much later was that Benjamin was inextricably tied in with my father's commercial arrangements, and that my entire future would play out because of a deal that the two struck without my knowledge but for the mutual benefit of all three of us.

I sensed that my father was bitterly disappointed in my lack of interest in the life of commerce that he lived…I simply didn't measure up to his expectations. Consequently, I knew that I couldn't continue working at the shop indefinitely; even though my father would have allowed me to do so in a menial capacity, it was far too painful for both of us to live the lie that I might some day fit in and be successful.

One day when Benjamin delivered some finished items to the shop, I was admiring one particularly beautiful leather pouch that he had made. "Would you like to learn how to make items like this?" he asked. "What do you mean?" I stammered. He replied "I'm getting older and have more orders than I can comfortably produce. I need an apprentice, and I would like it to be you. When I die, the business will be yours. What do you say?" I was dumbfounded at first, but the idea really appealed to me. Here was a graceful way out of the dead-end role I was in at the shop. While father might be disappointed, he would undoubtedly also be relieved that he no longer had me to contend with every day.

Benjamin continued: "There's a room behind the shop where I sleep. It's big enough for both of us. It gets pretty lonely at times, and we'd have each other to talk to. I think you'd make a fine artisan, especially since there's such a strong spiritual dimension to creating something beautiful with your own hands. I really want you to join me. Please." It never occurred to me to ask about wages, cost of food, or any other practical matter. Benjamin's reference to a "spiritual dimension" touched me deeply, and because of the unexpected tears in my eyes, I wordlessly nodded my assent. Benjamin smiled broadly. My tears were tears of relief, relief that I was finally out of the commercial trap that was making me so unhappy. With Benjamin, I could live a simple, unobtrusive life, and I sensed that I would have the time and freedom to pursue my spiritual growth as well.

My mother did not take the news well. Because I was her first-born, I held a special place in her heart, especially since I openly showed my love and respect for her. Furthermore, because I was sensitive and lacked the assertiveness and self-esteem of my father and my brother, she felt a special need to worry about me and to protect me. I assured her I would be fine, I wouldn't be far away, and I would visit often.

We made an agreement that each week I would come for dinner. I would bring my dirty clothes and pick up clean ones. Mother would also prepare sacks of groceries, fresh fruits and vegetables, wine, olive oil, and an assortment of other foodstuffs. There was always enough for both Benjamin and me. It was a wonderful, stress-free arrangement.

Benjamin was a balm for my soul, a true life-saver in every sense of the word. We prayed together frequently during the day. He patiently began to teach me the art of leather-working, sharing the not-widely-known techniques that made his work so beautiful and valuable. He graciously allowed me to slip away at times to hear a particularly gifted teacher at the temple, and he encouraged me to earnestly pursue my religious and spiritual studies. We sometimes talked long into the night, and I discovered that he was a sincere seeker of the truth and of God. I had found a permanent home.

THE ARRANGEMENT

After a few years of working with Benjamin, he finally revealed my father's part in my becoming a leather-working apprentice. It seems that my father had devised an ingenious scheme for increasing his wealth and power by controlling the best artisans of the city.

Father would watch closely and identify the most promising apprentices in each of the major trades. He would then offer to set them up with their own shops in exchange for a lifelong share of their income. This was very appealing to a young apprentice with no financial means; father would provide a shop, tools, raw materials, and start-up funds for the enterprise. Also, he would commit to become a major purchaser of the apprentice's output, as long as it was of the highest quality and could be bought at wholesale prices.

So the leading apprentices of the city, in every major trade, became quasi-indentured servants to Jacob, selling their best works of beauty to him at a significant discount and then giving him part of their earning as well. Benjamin gladly participated fully.

But it went further. In Benjamin's case, father had negotiated an agreement whereby Benjamin only paid me a portion of what was considered a fair wage. The remaining portion was given to father, who promised to save the money in a special fund for my future well-being. So the sack of coins that father later gave me for a wedding gift was actually money that I had earned and Benjamin had tithed. An ingenious scheme indeed!

RACHEL

After several years of a peaceful and satisfying life with Benjamin, things changed dramatically when I met Rachel. Until then, I had had little interest in women, preferring instead to pursue my religious studies while learning the leather-working trade.

Part of my work was to accompany Benjamin to the home of Reuben the tanner. Benjamin and Reuben liked each other and had been business associates for many years. Reuben withheld the finest leather from his display table and saved it for Benjamin. Benjamin paid him a slight premium for the highest-quality tanned hides, and both men were pleased with the arrangement, especially since Reuben admired Benjamin's work.

Reuben was a widower, and Rachel was his only daughter. Often when we visited Reuben for more tanned hides, we would sit in the shade and talk, and Rachel would bring us a cool drink of water from the nearby spring.

I never planned to court a woman and to marry, but to my astonishment I felt a deep and powerful attraction to this woman. I could not keep from frequently glancing at her when she wasn't looking, and some kind of a massive kinetic energy began to form in my heart. When I saw her, things happened inside of me that I couldn't explain, and sparks seem to arc between myself and her. Remarkably, Rachel seemed to be feeling the same thing. I started finding reasons to visit Reuben's shop more often, and Rachel was always there.

I now suspect that everyone was well aware of what was happening, perhaps even before Rachel and I even understood it fully. It wasn't long before I was deeply in love with her, and she with me. This was a time of parentally-arranged marriages, but since I didn't want to involve my parents, I asked Benjamin to approach Reuben to ask for Rachel's hand for me. Benjamin was delighted to do so.

It was a hard decision for Reuben. He would be losing his daughter, his companion, and his housekeeper and cook. However, he was a good man, and he realized that sooner or later someone would ask for Rachel in marriage. Further, he also had intricate business dealings with my father, and he guessed (wrongly) that I might someday inherit a large fortune. Finally, he found it impossible to turn down Benjamin, his best friend. And so he consented to our engagement, and a betrothal date was set for the following year.

I knew Benjamin to be a good man, but his outpouring of love and generosity astounded me. He insisted on adding a small room to his shop for himself, and gave Rachel and I the large living area for ourselves. My mother insisted on giving Rachel a wedding dress and other nice clothing. We eschewed the wedding my parents would have liked, and instead were married by a temple priest I admired, named Zechariah. Rachel had a favored cousin named Myriam, and she and Aaron were our witnesses. My mother and father and Benjamin and Reuben were the only other guests in attendance. My parents gave a dinner in our honor, and provided a room for our wedding night. Father gave me a large sack of coins as a wedding gift, which I sadly needed much sooner than expected.

Our life was indeed idyllic. Though my wages were meager, my parents provided food and clothing so we had few temporal needs and no financial worries. Rachel kept house for Benjamin and me, and we frequently invited Reuben to join us for evening dinner. I was able to both work and also spend time at the temple. Life was beautiful indeed.

Within a few months, Rachel became pregnant and began to blossom. She had been a radiant bride and was now even more radiant as a mother-to-be. I didn't know anyone could love another as much as I loved her. I awaited our child with great anticipation.

When the time arrived, we summoned the midwife and the process began. Shortly after, the midwife shouted instructions to summon the doctors immediately. I ran as fast as I could and found a doctor who was willing to come help us. But by the time we returned, matters had taken a turn for the worse. There was nothing that the doctor could do, and I could only hold Rachel and my new son as they both died in my arms. I wept uncontrollably.

My grief lasted for years. My mother tried to console me, but without success. Without Benjamin and Reuben, I would have probably ended my life. Instead, they shared my loss and allowed me to grieve in a full, sustained manner. I resolved never to love again.

From that day forward, life was a long, dull, tedious process of unfulfilling work and endless depression. All of the joy of living had gone out of me. My visits to the temple became less frequent because I had little desire to learn more about a God who would allow such a terrible, painful thing to happen to me, to us. Life seemed over for me.

ZECHARIAH

Zechariah was truly my salvation, both literally and figuratively. I had admired him from afar in the temple. He was a quiet man who spoke little, but when he did speak, his words were full of wisdom and regard for the Lord, and everyone listened carefully.

Zechariah lived in Ein Kerem, a short distance outside of the city gates, and his journeys to the temple took him by our leather-working shop. He recognized me from the times I sat in the background and listened to the teachers, so when time permitted, he would stop and talk to me. I was so impressed with his devoutness and his teaching that when the time came, I approached him and asked him to officiate at Rachel and my wedding, which he had done.

After the death of Rachel and my newborn son, Zechariah made a point of visiting more often and staying longer. He spoke with authority about the Lord having a plan for me, and that losing Rachel and my son were part of the plan, albeit a very painful part. He shared that he and his wife, Elizabeth, also lived a life of sadness because Elizabeth was without child, but they strove to remain faithful to the Lord and his plan of salvation.

I looked forward to Zechariah's visits, and I began to go with him on the days he served at the temple. He was obviously a holy man, and I was inspired by his witness. I would wait for him in the temple while he fulfilled his priestly duties, and we would then talk as we left the temple and journeyed back to the leather-working shop, where we would part.

One such day started out like all others, with Zechariah and me walking to the temple together. I waited outside as usual, sitting in the background near the rear of the crowd of worshippers as I always did. When Zechariah emerged from the inner sanctuary of the temple, pandemonium broke out among the crowd.

Zechariah, already an elderly man, could hardly function. He was unbelievably pale and he tottered as he walked. It appeared that he was visibly frightened, and the crowd speculated that he had seen a ghost. He was unable to answer the myriad of questions asked of him, and instead wended his way through the crowd to where I was waiting.

I took his arm and steadied him, and together we left the temple and began to walk to the leather-working shop. He pointed to his mouth and shook his head back and forth sideways, indicating that he could not talk. When we reached the shop, I gave him some water, which seemed to revive him. He bent down and wrote in the dust: "I've received great news. God is indeed good. I must go home now." I began to accompany him to Ein Kerem but he motioned me back to the shop, indicating that he was all right.

Zechariah stopped coming to the temple, so every so often I journeyed to Ein Kerem to see him. He was mute but obviously very happy. On one occasion I met his wife's young cousin, Mary, who radiated beauty and peace and had a presence about her that was unforgettable. It was during that visit that Zechariah pointed to his wife's stomach and smiled; it was obvious that after a long wait, Elizabeth would bear them a child.

When the child was born, the couple broke with tradition and named him John, despite the criticism of their neighbors and friends. Faced with the questioning and unable to speak, Zechariah asked for a tablet and wrote "His name is John," which ended the debate. It also ended his muteness; Zechariah broke out into a canticle of praise to the Lord that profoundly affected all who heard it, and that left them questioning the mystery of it all.

A few weeks later, Zechariah appeared at the leatherworking shop and asked me to accompany him to the temple. He respectfully asked Benjamin if he could keep me away from the shop for an extended period of time, and Benjamin readily agreed. We set off.

When we got to the temple, Zechariah led me to a small, private anteroom with a portico overlooking the city. The room was shaded and blessed with a cooling breeze. Zechariah had obviously chosen it carefully. "I have great news for your ears only," Zechariah began. "Salvation has come to us during our lifetimes. Praised be the holy Lord."

I looked at him quizzically. "I don't understand what you're saying." "The Messiah whom we've awaited will be born soon, and you will witness his greatness," he said. "How do you know this?" I said, already beginning to doubt his word. "Keep an open mind and I will explain it all. It's important that you believe what I tell you," he replied.

"When I was in the inner sanctuary some months ago, an angel appeared to me with astounding news.

Because I doubted, I was struck mute until it came to pass," he said.

"The angel told me that after a life of barrenness, Elizabeth would become pregnant in her old age. Further, the angel told me that this son should be called John, and that he would be a great man, and the forerunner and precursor of the Messiah who would come after him. Imagine, my son announcing the coming of the Lord. How blest we are!"

I looked at Zechariah with doubt in my heart. He obviously believed what he was saying, but I wasn't so sure. If it wasn't for my great respect and fondness for the man, I would have entirely dismissed what he was saying. "I can see you are struggling to believe," he said; "I struggled too. It seems so incredulous, so unreal, so unbelievable. But I have come to believe, and you will also. Let me tell you more about what has transpired."

He then told me about Elizabeth's cousin, Mary of Nazareth, also receiving a message from an angel announcing that she would be the mother of the Messiah. "The Mary I met?" I asked. "Yes," Zechariah said. "And upon hearing that Elizabeth was pregnant, she walked for several days from Nazareth to Ein Kerem to be of service to her cousin. Up until then, Elizabeth had felt no stirrings of her baby and was very fearful that she would deliver a stillborn child, but when the two of them met, the baby in Elizabeth's womb leapt uncontrollably with joy. Mary then sang a beautiful song of praise to God that was clearly inspired by the Spirit. This all happened, David, please believe me."

"This is all too incredible to be made up, David" he continued, "all too incredible and too wonderful and too unusual to be a lie. It's really happening, and the Messiah is coming!"

Conflicting sentiments of belief and doubt raced through my mind. Zechariah continued with his persuasive revelation. "Since being struck dumb I have spent several months studying the prophets. So far, everything is happening exactly as prophesied. If the prophecies are true and accurate, the Messiah should be born in Bethlehem, even though Mary and Joseph, her husband, live in Nazareth. We can only wait and see."

I thought back to when I met Mary at the home of Elizabeth and Zechariah in Ein Kerem, how plain and yet surreal she was, her peaceful countenance and demeanor, her mature willingness to be of service to her cousin, and now, if Zechariah was to be believed, her calm acceptance of the greatest news and the subsequent greatest event in Jewish history.

"Mary stayed with us for three months, and during that time she shared that she still was a virgin who had not known man, but rather that the Messiah was the product of the workings of the Holy Spirit within her. She was so prayerful, so willing to serve God and serve us, so open to whatever God had in store for her we could not help but believe her."

Zechariah and I talked at much greater length, until the sun began to set in the west. "I must hurry home," he said, "but we will talk again soon. You will have many questions, and we can explore them together. I am not asking you to blindly believe, but rather to keep your eyes open and stay awake so that you might intimately witness and be a part of salvation history as it unfolds before our very eyes." With that he rose and we traveled back to the leather-working shop together. He whispered "Shalom" in my ear as we parted.

ALONE

About this time, Reuben died, with Benjamin and me at his bedside. A short while later, the time I was dreading finally arrived. Benjamin contracted some kind of lung infection and became deathly ill. I had spent part of my father's sack of coins on doctors at the time of Rachel's death, and now I spent the rest on doctors and medicines for Benjamin. I sat by his bedside night and day ministering to him, but to no avail.

The fever worsened, and Benjamin slipped in and out of consciousness. During one period of clarity, he told me that the shop, the tools, and almost everything he had belonged to my father, but I was welcome to keep everything and use it unless my father wanted it returned. I was deeply moved and I laid my head on his chest and sobbed while listening to his rasping struggle for breath. I assured him that I loved him and would never forget him, and that his memory would be in all of the leather work I produced.

Shortly thereafter he asked me to pray for him and with him, and as I commended his spirit to a good and loving God, he drew his last breath and died peacefully in my arms.

For the first time in my life, I felt totally alone. Other than an occasional visit with my mother, I had no one except Zechariah in my life—no one to care about, and no one to care about me. I became a recluse, doing just enough leather work to keep my father and my other customers satisfied. Other than that, I sat in the dark, alone and depressed.

THE BIRTHDAY SURPRISE

Shortly before my thirtieth birthday, one of my father's servants appeared at the leather-working shop, informing me that I should be at my father's house on the eve of my birthday, and that I should expect to spend the night and part of the next day there. The news was delivered as more of an order than a request, and it was the first time my father had shown any interest in seeing me on my birthday since I had left home.

I dutifully arrived on the eve of my birthday and was immediately treated to a haircut, manicure and warm bath, followed by my favorite meal of goat meat roasted in eggplant. After a surprising evening of conviviality with my father, mother and brother, I was shown to my old bedroom which had been freshly appointed with beautiful linens. After a good night's sleep in a feather bed I was awoken by a servant and escorted to breakfast, which I ate alone. Shortly thereafter, I was given another warm bath and then dressed in beautiful, very expensive yet unobtrusive clothing. "Understated elegance," I called it.

At that point, my father appeared and sat on the edge of the bed. "I haven't been much of a father for you because I wanted to live my life vicariously through you, and it didn't work out. I wanted you to be the son of my dreams, but you didn't have the calling, the desire, or the aptitude to live the life I had mapped out for you." I sensed that he was near to tears as he spoke, something I had never seen before.

"I honor the path you have chosen for your life, and I want to give you something that I hope will bless you richly."

He stood up, drew me up out of my chair, and embraced me. "I'm sorry I wasn't a father for you, but I hope this will make up for my failure in some small way. Come with me and see what life now has in store for you. I pray that you will value what I have done."

I followed him out of the house and down the street toward the temple. I felt out of character in my splendid clothes and my gold-embroidered prayer shawl, and I wondered why my mother and brother weren't accompanying us. I was soon to find out.

We passed the temple proper and arrived at the meeting place of the Sanhedrin, where we were welcomed and ushered in by the door attendants. The entire Sanhedrin had been assembled, and I stood in awe as I gazed upon the most powerful religious leaders of Israel, all in one room. I recognized many of these men from the years I had spent watching them discuss and debate the scriptures, and many recognized me as well.

The head of the Sanhedrin spoke out in a booming voice: "Welcome, Jacob, and welcome, David, son of Jacob. We are blest by your presence here." Jacob bowed his head in respectful acknowledgment, and I followed suit. "David, we have followed your growth in your own spirituality and in your knowledge of our religion, and we have eagerly awaited your 30th birthday so that we might formalize our regard for you. If it be your wish, we ask you to step forward so that we might install you as an Elder, the youngest Elder to ever grace our august assembly. Do you wish to receive this honor?"

I was dumbfounded and paralyzed where I stood, but Jacob gave me an imperceptible nudge from behind, and I stepped forward to be inaugurated. The consecration ceremony was long and immensely rich in liturgical symbolism. The chamber was filled with the odor of burning incense and cedar, and the incantations sung by the assembly were moving indeed. Each member individually approached me, prayed for me with hands outstretched over my head, and then gave me the symbolic kiss of peace on both cheeks. When it was over, I was exhilarated and exhausted at the same time, and I stood numbly as the members exited pass me, wishing me welcome and blessings in my new role.

I looked at my father and realized immediately that he had arranged all of this, no doubt with the disbursement of many heavy sacks of coins in the proper pockets. I realized that he had cleverly found a way to further honor himself and his family while still giving me a new purpose that intrigued and honored me as well, while also frightening me greatly.

Despite my father's questionable motives, I was nevertheless grateful for the lengths to which he had gone to gift me. I realized that I lacked all of the basic requirements of being an Elder, such as wisdom, the ability to think on one's feet and to discuss and debate extemporaneously, a close relationship with God, and a thirst for the power and prestige that being a member of the Sanhedrin brought with it. I would likely be nothing more than a silent observer in the proceedings, and everyone including myself knew that, but just to be present for the inner workings of this august body excited me greatly. I thanked my father with a deferential embrace, and we proceeded home in silence.

BETHLEHEM

The edict came down from the Romans that every Jewish citizen must return to the town of their ancestry to register for a nationwide census. This was only a minor annoyance for me, since Bethlehem was only a short distance away from the leather-working shop.

The inn-keeper knew my father and had also heard of my new status as an Elder, so I was given one of the few private rooms in the inn at a large discount from the normal price. After my favorite meal of goat's meat and marinated eggplant, I retired to my room and went to sleep quickly. I was disturbed by pounding on the inn door and voices telling the intruders to go away because there was no room left, but I quickly went back to sleep.

Later I was awakened again by a bright light shining in my window from overhead, and a voice moaning in pain in the barnyard. I donned my elder robes and hurried out to investigate, and I discovered a couple in the stable, with the woman obviously in the throes of childbirth. A maid-servant arrived at the same time, carrying hot water and clothing. The pregnant woman clutched my arm with one of her hands, and her husband's arm with her other hand, and the maid-servant served as a midwife. I was terrified. I had never gotten over the death of Rachel, my wife, during childbirth and also the death of my son less than an hour later. Flashbacks of me holding both Rachel and the infant for a few moments while

Rachel bled to death and the infant ceased breathing now came back to me like a nightmare and I had all I could do to keep my wits about me.

In a respite from her unconscionable labor pains, the woman, sensing my panic, turned to me and smiled, saying "It will be all right, Elder David, this is all a part of God's plan. The baby and I will be fine. You are blessed to be here watching this special child's birth." Despite her words, I didn't yet grasp the significance of what was taking place.

The maid-servant delivered the squalling baby boy. We were all alone, just the four of us. When the baby emerged, the maid-servant cut the umbilical cord and handed the baby to me. My beautiful elder robes were soon blood-stained, but the baby and his mother were alive and doing well. Memories of the loss of Rachel and my son kept flooding into my mind, and I stood weeping as I held the newborn infant, full of grief at the loss I experienced so many years ago, and of the life of loneliness I had lived since then, devoid of the love and companionship that I still wanted so badly. I continued to cradle the now peaceful infant in my arms while the man cared for his wife. A powerful sensation came over me, and I realized I was now part of a very grace-filled event.

The maid-servant was wonderful, bringing soap, warm water, and healing ointment, and then disappearing into the inn with bloodied clothes and towels and reappearing with clean ones. She seemed to be everywhere at once and she obviously knew exactly what was needed at every moment. She looked vaguely familiar, but I couldn't place her.

Nor could I place the new mother right away, until she was cleaned up and re-dressed in clean garments. She sat up and gestured to me to hand her the newborn baby. As she did so, I looked into her eyes and realized that it was Mary, Elizabeth's cousin from Nazareth.

Zechariah's words came rushing into my mind; "He's supposed to be born in Bethlehem, even though Mary and Joseph live in Nazareth. Let's wait to see what happens."

Could it be that I was the first to hold the Messiah, the Son of God? I was dumbstruck with the realization, but I had little time to ponder it, because visitors started arriving. The bright light that had awakened me now hovered directly overhead, and soon shepherds came and announced that they were summoned at the direction of angels.

They knelt to worship the new Savior with wonder and awe. An angelic choir sang beautiful "Hosannas" and "Alleluias" overhead, and the bright light from the star illuminated everything. Before long, three noblemen arrived on dromedaries from distant countries, paid homage on their knees to the new child, and left precious gifts for him.

After everyone had left, the maid-servant re-appeared carrying warm drinks for the exhausted couple and for me. "This is 'bravitzka'," she said. "It is my mother's health-filled concoction, and it will restore your energy and give you plentiful milk for the baby. I will keep a batch of it warming near the oven fire, and please come and get more whenever you need it. Also, let me know if there's anything more I can do for you." Then I spoke to the couple: "Tomorrow I am leaving. Move into my private room in the inn which is paid for. It is my gift to you and the infant. I am surely privileged to be present at the birth of my Lord." They both smiled, blessed me, and whispered "shalom," and I returned to my room in the inn, forever changed by the unprecedented experience.

GLAD TIDINGS

All night I thought about the maid-servant. I knew that we had met, but I couldn't place where or when. She certainly had been magnificent in her caring for the pregnant couple, and I wanted to thank her on their behalf. Very early the next morning, I went looking for her and she was already in the kitchen when I entered. She handed me a platter of freshly baked food. "Please take this out to our new friends," she said, "they will need it for what they will soon face." I took the food to Mary and Joseph, and they were grateful beyond measure. I asked if I might hold the sleeping infant, and Mary smilingly nodded her assent. I was now far more conscious than before that I might be holding the Savior of the world. I returned the sleeping baby boy and gave Mary and Joseph my first Elder blessings. It felt wonderful. I gave them the coins I had left and bid them a fond farewell.

I returned to the kitchen to pursue the identity of the maid-servant, but she had disappeared and was nowhere to be found. Not finding her, I left the inn and headed directly to Ein Kerem. I found Zechariah sitting in the shade, rocking his six-month-old son. I commented on the infant's flaming red hair. "I don't know where he gets it from," Zechariah said laughingly, "but it certainly matches his fiery, passionate disposition."

I then began to tell Zechariah about all that had transpired, but he stopped me and called for Elizabeth to join us so that she could hear my account as well. "Start over and don't skip a single thing," he instructed, "every little detail is important to Elizabeth and me."

I spent the next several hours recounting all that I had seen, including the star, the shepherds, the magi, the maid-servant, and everything else of which I could think. When I was done, Zechariah began citing the prophecies regarding the Messiah, including Micah, Isaiah, and several others. All of them had been completely and accurately fulfilled in the events at Bethlehem. If I had any vestigial doubts about the identity of the new infant, they were completely dissolved by Zechariah's learned discourse. I had witnessed the birth of the Messiah, the Savior, the Christ, and I had held him in my arms!

Several days later, Zechariah came rushing into my shop. "Hurry," he said, "Mary and Joseph are on their way to the temple to present the infant to God. I want to witness it." I held Zechariah's arm and we walked as fast as we could to the temple. Joseph was in the process of buying a pair of doves, and I recognized the coin purse that I had given the couple as the purse from which he extracted the few coins I had been able to spare.

The presentation was quiet and simple. An elderly holy man named Simeon took the infant in his arms and proph-esied about him. Simeon had been promised by God that he would not die until he saw the Redeemer. He proclaimed "Now, Master, you can dismiss your servant in peace, for you have fulfilled your word." Likewise, a saintly woman named Anna also prophesied about him, and everyone blessed him and praised the Lord as he was consecrated to God as the first-born of Mary and Joseph. The couple took their leave to return to the inn for a few more days of rest and recu-peration. I tried to visit them the next day, but they had unexpectedly left and had vanished without a trace.

REUNION

Many years later I was working in my shop when a strange impulse came over me, prompting me to go to the temple. It was highly unusual for me to go to the temple on a workday, and it would entail bathing and donning my Elder garments. However, the intuition would not go away, but rather grew stronger, so I ceased working and went.

When I got to the men's section of the temple, a large crowd had gathered in a shaded corner. I looked over the heads of those in front of me, and I beheld a young man of eleven or twelve discoursing with the teachers. Because I was older, one of the younger Pharisees caught my attention and motioned me to a vacant bench near to the youth.

In no time I became transfixed with the wisdom coming from the young man's mouth. He had a clearer understanding of the historical and spiritual implications of scripture than anyone else I had ever heard, even Zechariah. And his exposition of the deeper mysteries and meanings of various passages astounded everyone, myself included.

I sat for the entire day, listening to his brilliance. "Who is he?" I asked another Elder. "He is Jesus, from Nazareth, the son of a carpenter. I don't know where he got such deep knowledge of these matters. Certainly not at a workbench!" Once I heard the name Jesus, from Nazareth, I knew the truth, and for the next two days I sat near him and was totally absorbed in what the young man had to say. I had again met Jesus, Messiah!

ENLIGHTENMENT

Life would never be the same, although my daily routine at the leather-working shop became tedious and unfulfilling. For some reason, I kept wondering about the identity of the maid-servant at the inn in Bethlehem, and despite fairly frequent rumination about her, I couldn't place who she was for a long time. Because there was dim light in the stable and we were both preoccupied with the birthing process, I never got a really good look at her, but her essence of caring, service, and inner beauty had touched me deeply.

Then one night, while dozing off to sleep, I made the connection. The maid-servant was Myriam, Rachel's cousin who had witnessed our marriage so many years ago. What a coincidence, I thought, that we should meet again in such an unusual circumstance. Her image continued to reappear in my mind at odd times, and I never again forgot her.

I escaped from the shop whenever my work allowed. At times I went to the temple, but more often I journeyed to Ein Kerem. Zechariah had grown quite feeble, but his mind was still brilliantly clear, and we spent hours with him conveying to me his extensive grasp of the scriptures, and especially of the prophecies surrounding the Messiah.

I tried to find inconsistencies between the prophecies and the reality of Jesus' birth, but I could not do so. Zechariah had an answer for every doubt I expressed, and as time went on, I gained firm and absolute assurance in my own mind that Jesus was the Messiah.

From his earliest days, John, Zechariah's red-headed son, showed a surprisingly strong interest in our discussions, and often sat with us for hours. At times, he would crawl up on his father's lap or my lap but at other times he would sit on the ground at our feet.

But Zechariah didn't limit his teaching to scripture study. Because of his sage advice, I learned much about the workings of the Sanhedrin, including the politics, the cliques, the voting blocs, and the behind-the-scenes machinations that constituted the way in which the entire Jewish state was really governed. I gained much more understanding and became a much more effective Sanhedrin member as a result of Zechariah's wisdom.

Because of Zechariah, both my knowledge of the Lord and my love for Him blossomed. My entire life revolved around the study and understanding of scripture. I saw clearly that for millennia, mankind's writings and oral pronouncements had pointed to the coming of the Messiah. I began to overcome my timidity and speak up at the temple during debates. In essence, I took over Zechariah's role; I didn't speak much, but when I did my viewpoints seemed to carry weight with the other members. I was respected.

Without Zechariah, my life would have been totally empty. He was everything for me: father, brother, teacher, mentor, and role model. He believed in me and invested himself fully in passing on everything he knew to me. He certainly lived the canticle he recited upon the birth of his son, when he proclaimed: "We should serve him devoutly and through all our days be holy in his sight." Zechariah surely was a true servant of God.

ALONE

It seemed that the few remaining people in my life all left me in short order. My father had died a few years previous, and now my mother passed away as well. I would see my brother, Aaron, when I delivered leather goods to his shop, but we had nothing in common and virtually no relationship beyond polite and brief verbal exchanges.

The greatest loss was that of Elizabeth and Zechariah. Elizabeth died quietly in her sleep, and Zechariah followed her the next morning. Not even death could separate this beautiful couple, who had served as my surrogate parents and truly saved me from a life of emptiness, loneliness, and despair. And now they were both gone. The red-headed John, now an adolescent, promptly left Ein Kerem and went to live with the Essenes near the Dead Sea. There was no one left for me to talk to, not a single solitary soul.

Shortly before he died, and with rapidly failing eyesight, Zechariah had given me his extensive collection of sacred scrolls. My life was now reduced to working leather, going to the temple, and devoting countless hours to studying those scrolls. They turned out to be a God-send; without them, my life would have been totally empty, but with them, I could immerse myself in the history of the Jewish people and their on-again-off-again relationship with God. I gained an ever-clearer understanding of salvation history, and while most Jews expected a Messiah to come with might and power, I saw that Isaiah's description of a humble servant who must ultimately suffer and die would be the reality.

THE SIGHTING

Many years passed and I had had no word of the whereabouts of John or of his cousin, Jesus. I was essentially a hermit in my shop, rarely venturing out except to go to the temple or buy a small amount of food to eat. I was now in my early sixties, and I had already lived much longer than anyone could reasonably expect. I started to wish for death as an escape from the painful void in which I existed. "Let me die" was my prayer.

All that changed one day when I was in the temple. News spread like wildfire that there was some red-headed firebrand preaching and baptizing in a remote area of Judea near the river Jordan. As I learned more about this independent, fiercely confrontational crusader, I suspected that it might be Zechariah's son, John, but I did not yet connect John as the precursor of Jesus, even though that truth was suggested in the scriptures.

So one day, long before sunrise, I set out to see if I could find John. It was a grueling walk for me at my age, but my curiosity wouldn't let me rest until I made the journey. John wasn't hard to find; multitudes of people were on the path ahead of me, all bent on hearing the words of this latest prophet. We eventually reached the Jordan River, not much more than a large stream, and there was John in the water, his camel-hair clothes girt around his loins, immersing people in the river while exhorting them to beg forgiveness for their sins and repent so that their souls might be ready for the coming of one greater than he, the Messiah.

Soldiers, tax collectors, and others all asked John for advice on how to live, and he freely gave them sound advice that revolved around treating others fairly and with compassion.

As was my wont, I stood at the back of the crowd and watched and listened intently. It was chaotic bedlam; hundreds of people were pushing and shoving to be next to be baptized, and John was attempting to serve them all while exhorting the remainder of the crowd to turn away from sin and toward a life lived according to the teachings of God.

In the midst of the frenzy, John suddenly stopped what he was doing and gazed at the shore, speechless and somewhat aghast. A small group of men was approaching, all apparently local laborers of one sort of another, but one man stood out because of the unusual way he carried himself, full of poise and calmness and assurance and peace. Regaining his composure, John nodded toward the group of men and said: "I am baptizing you with water, but there is one to come who is mightier than I. I am not fit to loosen his sandal strap. He will baptize you in the Holy Spirit and in fire."

The group of men approached John and, one by one, were immersed in the Jordan's waters. When the final one approached John, John was seen shaking his head back and forth in a vehement refusal, but the man spoke softly and convincingly to John, and John proceeded to humbly baptize him as well. I was astounded at what happened next. The skies seemed to open and a form like a dove descended over the man, and a voice from the sky was clearly heard to say: "You are my beloved Son. On you my favor rests."

EXPLOITATION

I was not blessed with a facile mind, and it usually takes some period of pondering before things make sense to me. Maybe I should have known that the "beloved Son" was Jesus, but I hadn't seen him since eighteen years ago, when he was but a youth. The truth finally dawned on me when I overheard a Scribe talking about the crowds flocking to John the Baptist. "Even the new rabbi, Jesus from Nazareth, got baptized," he said, "and many reported an eerie vision and a voice from the sky as he emerged from the water."

From that time forward, I tried to keep up with the rumors and gossip about this unusual man, and I eagerly awaited a chance to meet him in person. One day I was talking again with the same Scribe, and I mentioned my interest in meeting Jesus. "That man over there talking to the money changers might help you," he said, "he is a disciple of Jesus."

I approached the man, greeted him with a gesture of peace, and introduced myself. "What do you want?" he responded brusquely, not sharing his name nor wishing me peace in return. "I want to meet Jesus of Nazareth alone and in person," I replied. "It can be arranged," he responded; "be at the East Gate at daybreak, and bring thirty silver coins, which is the value of my time spent arranging for your meeting."

I nodded my head and walked away, stunned. It never occurred to me that meeting Jesus would cost far more than I had, but I numbly accepted the agreement without argument.

I quickly left the temple. There was only one place I might get such a significant amount of money, so I swallowed my pride and headed toward my brother's shop. He greeted me coolly and gave me a perfunctory kiss of peace. Without any further inquiry into my well-being, he got right to the point. "What do you want?" he asked.

"I would like to borrow thirty silver coins," I told him. "How soon can you pay them back?" he questioned. A myriad of clever answers swirled through my mind, but I always attempted to be an honest man, so I told him the truth: "It will take me a long time to repay you, and it's possible that I may never be able to earn that much money."

He questioned me further: "What do you want it for?" "There's a new teacher named Jesus of Nazareth, and I want to meet him," I responded. "Is the money for this Jesus?" my brother asked. "No, the money is for the intermediary who is setting up the meeting," I said. He snorted and curtly said: "It seems like an exorbitant amount of money just to set up a meeting between two people. How soon do you need the coins?" I looked down at the ground. Money had never been important to me before, and now I was having to beg for it. I stammered: "Right now, if you have it. The meeting is set up for tomorrow."

Aaron shook his head in disbelief. "Thirty silver coins just to meet an itinerant teacher. It doesn't make any sense to me," he added over his shoulder as he disappeared into the shop. When he returned, he was empty-handed. "I won't lend you the money," he said. I lowered my head in shame and disappointment, and started to turn and leave his shop.

His whole demeanor then changed and a slight smile appeared on his face. "In your entire life you have never asked me for anything, not even a legitimately fair price for your leatherwork. So I won't loan you the money, but instead I'll give it to you as a partial payback for all of the profits I've made on your beautiful leather products." And with that, he placed a bag of coins in my hand and hugged me warmly. "It doesn't make sense to me," he said, "but if it's that important to you, I will not refuse to help you."

I mumbled my thanks, tears streaming down my face, and turned to leave. "You're a good and holy man, David," he said. "Please say some prayers for me; I'm a sinner." I left his shop, humbled and grateful. Everything was now in place. I would meet Jesus.

Unable to sleep, I arose long before daybreak and headed toward the East Gate, my bag of coins safely tucked inside my best Elder robe, which I chose to wear for the occasion. As I approached the gate, a figure stepped out of the shadows, and panic gripped me. I had never given a thought to robbers, and here I was carrying a very large sum of money.

But the man was my contact. I heaved a sigh of relief. "Have you got the money?" he asked. I nodded my head. "I want it now," he said, "before we go anywhere." Without question, I drew the bag from inside my robe and handed it to him. He counted it carefully and nodded his head. "Thirty silver coins," he said, "and a bargain at that." He swiftly led the way across the Kidron Valley and up the Mount of Olives, passing by an olive grove called Gethsemane. My age was showing and I had all I could do to keep up.

THE MEETING

We approached the summit and came upon a figure silhouetted in the early dawn light. His face was lifted to the sky, and he was obviously deep in prayer. As we drew closer, I gestured to my guide to not bother Jesus but he instead announced "You have a visitor."

The first rays of daylight appeared behind Jesus, and I couldn't tell if the glow behind him emanated from him or from the sun. Jesus immediately rose, approached me, and giving me a warm kiss of peace, said "Shalom, Venerable Elder, you are welcome here."

I sat down near him on a flat stone, totally exhausted by the brisk climb uphill. My guide had had little concern for my age, and had struck a pace that was far too strenuous for me. Jesus observed all of this and said: "Catch your breath while you enjoy this beauty. Isn't this view magnificent?" Indeed it was. The spot had obviously been chosen with care. The first rays of sunlight were illuminating Jerusalem, and especially the temple, with highlights of gold interspersed with shadows of dark gray, providing a bas relief effect that was breathtaking. To the west we looked down on Bethany, where Jesus was staying, and then beyond Bethany to even more desolate stretches of desert beyond it.

We sat in silence, mesmerized by the sunrise creeping across the desert, sweeping over our heads, and illuminating the breathtakingly beautiful city. I felt no need to speak, and neither did Jesus. It was enough being in his presence, and I was content.

After a time, I spotted a wolf-like animal emerging from the desert and starting to climb toward us up the eastern slope. He was the most beautiful animal I had ever seen. He was sleek and muscular, in peak condition, with a lustrous coat of silver and black. My guide saw him too, and when the animal got close enough, he began throwing large stones at him. "What are you doing, Judas?" Jesus asked. "Amusing myself," Judas answered. "And what if you hit the animal?" Jesus asked quietly. "So what?" Judas responded. "You will hurt him," Jesus continued. "So what?" Judas countered again. "Stop throwing stones," Jesus directed, "I don't want one of God's creatures to be hurt."

Judas scowled at Jesus and wandered off. We continued to sit in silence. Shortly thereafter, Judas reappeared and announced that he was going back to Jerusalem. As he turned to leave, Jesus quietly instructed him "Give David back his money." Judas scowled at me with anger and contempt. "David didn't tell me about the money, Judas," Jesus said, "I already knew. As my disciple, I expect you to bring all sincere seekers to me, freely and without cost. This is your calling, to bring all people to me that they might be saved."

Judas removed my sack from an inner compartment of his tunic and dropped it on the ground in front of me. He started to stride away when Jesus' voice stopped him in his tracks. "Give David back all of his money, Judas, all of it." Judas now was enraged; he glared at Jesus while retrieving the rest of my coins from a hidden pocket, and he threw them disdainfully at my feet. "You'd better leave now, Judas" Jesus said, at which Judas stormed off, muttering profanities as he went. The beautiful animal had also disappeared.

Once we were alone, Jesus turned to me and asked: "Is there something I can do for you, David?" His question was so courteous, so caring, so compassionate that it caught me off guard. I thought awhile and then answered honestly: "I have had a strong desire to meet you. Beyond that, I don't know; I'm quite overwhelmed by finally getting to meet you."

"Re-meet me," he said with a smile, "you've already met me before." "That's correct," I responded, "but it was many years ago in the temple when you were a young man instructing some of the leading scriptural scholars in the land. They were spellbound." "And what about Bethlehem?", he asked, obviously relishing the repartee. He surprised me by referring to the night of his own birth. "Bethlehem," I responded. "That was truly a magical night. Singing, and light, and celebration in the cold." "And Myriam," he said, "with her bravitzka, and then Jerusalem a few days later," he added. "Yes," I said, "just the little circle of your parents, Simeon, Anna, and my friend Zechariah." He nodded.

I was now totally dumbfounded. He knew about my purse full of coins hidden in Judas' cloak, and he knew all about his birth and the days that followed. I didn't know how to continue, so I remained silent. He finally continued: "You were very kind to all of us."

"When you came back to the inn the day after my parents consecrated me to God in the temple as their first-born, we had already left, fleeing to Egypt. One of my parents' regrets was that they never had a chance to thank you for all you had done for them. So I'm thanking you on their behalf, Elder David." I nodded my acknowledgment.

We sat in silence a while longer, and then Jesus rose to leave. "I've got to go now, David," he announced, "the others will be looking for me. Why don't you think some more about what you want and what I might be able to do for you," he said with great tenderness, "and come back tomorrow if you would like to talk some more." He hugged me with a kiss of peace, whispered "Shalom, Holy Elder," and left to go back to Bethany.

I sat there in the first rays of sunshine, the morning still cool and dewy and beautiful. Ever since my extended conversations with Zechariah I had firmly believed that Jesus was the Messiah, the Chosen One of God. So my meeting with Jesus had thrown me off balance. I expected him to be powerful, authoritarian, rigid, and righteous, but none of those attributes had been visible. Instead, I found him to be gentle, compassionate, understanding, loving and respectful. He had been direct and assertive with Judas, but even then he had appeared to be operating from a place of love, concern, and correction.

"Is this what God is supposed to be like?" I asked myself. I hadn't expected a humble servant, but as I sat there, many of Isaiah's prophecies came to mind, and I remembered that the Messiah would be characterized by love, compassion, and service to humankind. Compared to the God I thought I knew, the God I feared, Jesus was beautifully different: approachable, concerned, down-to-earth, and respectful. I couldn't wait to see him again.

I sat until almost midday, wanting to hold onto the aura of holiness and peace I had absorbed from Jesus. Finally, I slowly wended my way back down the mountain.

Back in Jerusalem, I went first to Aaron's shop. He greeted me warmly. I was surprised by his friendliness. I don't know what happened to effect the change that had come over him, but I was suddenly feeling a closeness to him that I had never felt before.

"I've come to return your silver coins," I said, "it turned out that I didn't need them." Aaron smiled. "You keep them," he said, "because some day you will need them. At the moment I can spare them without missing them at all; at a later time, I might not be able to give them to you no matter how urgent your need. So please keep them as my gift to you. Pray for me, and tell me more about this Jesus as you get to know him better."

I gave him the traditional kiss of peace and he returned it with feeling. "Shalom," we said to each other, and I hurried off. Next was the shop of Mortaci, my friend the tanner.

I purchased all of my leather from Mortaci, and we had had some serious talks about God, the meaning of life, death, the end-times, etc. I could trust him. I came to Mortaci because he knew a lot about animals, and I knew that he believed that when an animal appeared unexpectedly in one's life, there was symbolism and meaning to the meeting.

I told him about the wild animal, and he agreed that the description didn't fit any of the animals indigenous to the area. He thought for a long while, and then said: "If the animal approaches you peacefully, then the universe is sending you a guardian to direct you and to protect you against danger, and especially against unknown danger."

I was surprised with his interpretation, but as I looked at him, he continued: "I strongly believe this animal may be trying to approach you, and if so, that it has been sent to you. Stay open to the possibilities, and let it unfold as it is meant to be. Do not be afraid."

I was suddenly inspired with another thought. Seeing the discarded scraps of leather lying on the dusty floor, I asked if I might have some. "What for?", he asked, "surely not to make something to sell." "No," I replied, "I want to make something for myself." He assembled an armful of scraps, bound them up with a root cord, and handed them to me. "Bring the cord back," he said, "so I can reuse it. And good luck with your project."

Next I stopped at the shop of Gideon, the meat curer. I hardly could afford meat, so I rarely bought it and consequently I did not know Gideon well, so I was a bit apprehensive about my request. After greeting one another, he asked me: "What can I do for you today, Elder David?" "Do you have any meat scraps I could have?", I asked meekly. "Who are they for?" he queried. I hesitated. Telling the truth was always hard for me when I feared that the other person might not like what I had to say, but after an interior struggle, I always strove to tell the truth. "It's for a wild animal I'm trying to attract."

Gideon looked at me somewhat incredulously, but since he sensed how serious I was about my request, he responded: "I try to use every scrap of meat I have for resale, and when I have any pieces I can't dry and sell, I give them to my dog. But you are in luck; I have a small pile here, and my dog will never know that I gave you half of his supper."

Gideon took a large wet leaf from a bowl of water he kept for this purpose, wrapped the scraps of meat, and handed them to me. "Keep the leaf wet and in the shade," he said, "and the meat will last longer before it starts to spoil." I thanked him warmly and left.

My own words hit me as I walked down the dusty path: "I want to attract a wild animal," I had said. The revelation to myself came as a shock, and I asked myself: "Why do I want to attract this potentially dangerous animal? What's going on inside of me?"

I returned to my shop and proceeded to bury the sack of coins under a large rock in the shop foundation. Then I began cutting and assembling the scraps of leather, and while I worked, I was fully absorbed with thoughts about the beautiful animal, and also with Jesus' suggestion that I wanted more than just to meet him. As dusk approached, the feeling inside me grew stronger and stronger that he was right; I wanted something much more than just to meet him, but until his pointed questioning, I hadn't dug deep enough inside myself to discover that desire. Or perhaps more truthfully, I had been afraid to unearth and touch the strong need deep within me. And the animal was part of it, I knew.

I was awake most of the night, thinking about the day's encounter, about Jesus and Judas, and the wolf-like animal, about what had been said, and perhaps more importantly, what hadn't been said. Jesus had a way of looking at me lovingly and seeing my soul. I suspected that even the most poised individual could become flustered in his presence. Because of his probing, I now knew what I wanted, and I was eager to share it with him.

BRAVITZKA

The night seemed never to end, and I finally rose long before dawn. For some reason, I eschewed my elder's clothing and instead put on the knee-length tunic I wore in the shop. I had turned the scraps of leather into a multi-compartmented over-the-shoulder carrying bag, and I was pleased with the result. I put the wet leaf containing the meat into the bag and set off in the dark, anticipating a morning of silence and peace in Jesus' company.

The dim light of a new moon was all that I had to guide my steps, and my failing eyesight slowed my progress. As I approached the gate of the city where I had met Judas the day before, I saw a figure step out into the faint light. Fear seized me; was it Judas bent on revenge for the previous day's event, or was it some thief about to try to steal my money? I was too close to turn back and too feeble to run away, so I continued on toward the gate.

"Shalom," the figure said. "I have something for the Master to nourish and strengthen him. Please take it to him." With that, the person whom I now identified as a woman handed me an olive-wood cup, full of a warm drink, and disappeared into the dark.

I groped my way down the steep eastern side of the Kidron Valley and up the even steeper eastern side, past Gethsemane and up toward the top of the Mount of Olives.

When I got almost there, I retrieved the meat scraps from my new carry-bag and placed them on a large flat rock that I would be able to see from my meeting place with Jesus.

I continued to the meeting spot, knowing that it was still dark and therefore suspecting that Jesus would not yet be there, but I was surprised to find him there already, his head again turned to the sky in prayer. As was my wont, I had not yet fathomed what had transpired with the woman and the cup of warm liquid, but the drink had an unusual aroma and I sensed that I had smelled it once before in the distant past. Beyond that, the significance of it didn't register, and instead I simply brought it to Jesus as requested.

"Shalom, Venerable Elder David," he said, arising to greet me with the kiss of peace. "Shalom," I responded, embracing him and handing him the cup. "You must have encountered Myriam," he noted, "she's always doing thoughtful things like this for me. Her bravitzka is a wonderful concoction, and only she knows how to make it." I then understood; Myriam, who was in Rachel and my wedding, and who was at Jesus' birth in Bethlehem, was now still doing supportive things for him. I was taken aback by this information, and questions began to race through my mind. "How did she know that I would be at the gate at that hour, and how did she know I was going to meet Jesus?"

Before I could ask Jesus about this, he was raising the beautiful wooden cup toward the sky with both hands and saying a quiet prayer of thanks and blessing to God. As he lowered the cup, he spread his hands apart and there was now a cup full of warm bravitzka in each of his hands. I gasped. He handed me a cup and I sipped the brew. It was at a perfect temperature, even though it had been exposed to the cool air for an hour. We sat savoring our bravitzka, and I realized something truly miraculous had occurred.

I now expected the same peaceful contemplation as he and I had shared the previous day, and we did in fact silently watch the first rays of dawn go from pink to red to orange and finally yellow. The myriad of changing colors bathing the city were magnificent, but the sand dunes rapidly changing hues in the desolate wilderness also caught our attention.

I was waiting for Jesus to ask me if I had determined if there was more that I wanted than just to have met him, especially since I had returned the second day, but when he broke the silence he surprised me with a significantly different line of questioning. "Please tell me your life story," he said. He caught me off guard. "You probably know all about my life already," I said, "and furthermore, there isn't really a lot to tell." "I do know all about your life," he responded, "but you don't. You see it as a series of unrelated events to which you reacted, whereas I see it as God's will for you unfolding in an orderly way."

I gulped. This wasn't going to be as easy or as pleasant as I had thought. I saw that I had no choice but to begin. "Well," I said, "I was the first-born child of a strong, domineering father, and a very submissive mother. Growing up, I was educated by a rabbi like many of the other more privileged boys in my neighborhood. My father hoped that I would succeed him in the family business, but I was an abject failure at business. I never measured up to his expectations, and his dreams for me were surely unrealized. My father gave the first-born birthright to my younger brother, who was good at business, and I didn't mind very much, because it took away the pressure on me. But the rabbi recognized my interest in religion and spent a lot of extra time with me, which I liked."

"Was the rabbi 'just another rabbi'?", Jesus asked. "No," I said, "he was the best religious teacher in the city. He only tutored a few students; it was a privilege to study under him."

"How did you feel about your father?" Jesus persisted. "I didn't want to be around him, because I felt like such a failure, and I sensed I had little worth in his eyes," I answered. "I was a huge disappointment. I avoided him and mostly did menial work in the back room of the shop. I escaped to the synagogue each day as soon as my work was done."

"Eventually he apprenticed me to a leather-worker named Benjamin. When Benjamin died, he left me his business. When I turned thirty, my father pulled some strings, reportedly doled out some bags of coins, collected on a few IOU's, and used his influence to have me named an elder, probably trying to enhance the family's prestige. Since then, I have sat quietly at Sanhedrin meetings and then retreated to my leather-working shop."

"You don't think much of your father, nor of yourself, do you, David?" Jesus remarked. I looked down and swallowed hard. No answer came readily to mind, so I stayed silent. Jesus continued: "Do you mind if I ask you a few questions?" I hesitated and then slowly responded: "I guess not," even though I felt apprehension quickly rising in my stomach.

"Let's talk about your father, first" Jesus said. "Is it possible that he recognized early that you didn't have an aptitude for business, but preferred religious studies instead? And is it also possible that it wasn't just a coincidence that you studied under the very best rabbi?"

I was trying to think of an answer, but Jesus continued the questioning. "Is it possible that the rabbi spent many extra hours with you, not just because he liked you, and not just because you were an apt student, but also because your father paid him handsomely to do so? Is it also possible that your father made it easy for you to go to the synagogue often, guilt-free, while your brother worked long hours at the shop?"

I was in shock, feeling very much on the defensive. I had never given my father any credit for any of these events, and surely hadn't given him the benefit of a doubt as to his motives. I was beginning to wonder whether I had misjudged my father's intentions.

Jesus was unrelenting in his questioning. "As a young man in the back-room of your father's shop, what kind of a life did you yearn for?" "I wanted to work just enough in a quiet, stress-free environment so that I could live simply, and beyond that, I wanted to pursue my religious studies intensely," I responded. "And so do you think your father's choice of Benjamin was mere caprice or without strategic forethought?" Jesus asked.

"Think about it, David. With Benjamin, you were with a holy, prayerful man who allowed you the freedom of your religious studies, who prayed with you, who allowed you into his home as his own son, who moved out of his own living quarters when you got married, and who engaged you in long discussions about all of the critical issues of human existence and about relationship with God. Was it a coincidence that you were placed in such an environment, or was your father lovingly thoughtful in the matter?"

I started to weep. I had judged my father very harshly, and now Jesus had raised the possibility that my father had loved me deeply and cared about my well-being, but perhaps was unable to express it verbally but instead did extremely loving things for me. "Forgive me, father," I said through choking sobs, "I have done you a great wrong."

Jesus allowed me to weep in sorrow for a long time. It was now fully light, and I looked at the beautiful city through tear-filled eyes. Eventually, Jesus spoke again. "What about Zechariah?", he said, "you didn't even mention Zechariah. Do you think that it was just a coincidence that Zechariah came into your life, taught and mentored you, spent countless hours explaining the prophecies, and introduced you to my parents, to Simeon, to Anna?"

I looked at the ground, speechless. He was right, painfully right. "And one more thing," he added: "You said you sit quietly at Sanhedrin meetings and then return to the leather shop. I tell you that you are one of the finest scripture scholars in this country, and you are recognized as such by everyone except yourself. On the few occasions when you speak, you have wonderful insight and wisdom to provide, and everyone is edified. So why are you hiding your light under a bushel and not sharing your gifts? Are you going to die without making the contribution to humankind that God wants you to make?"

Jesus continued: "David, your life has been a rich preparation, orchestrated by God directly and also by God through your father, Benjamin, Zechariah, and many others. Even the death of Rachel and your son, no matter how painful, was a preparation."

"Don't you see, David, there is an ongoing saga here, right up to this minute, a story of preparation for something bigger. God's hand has been in your life all along, and you have cooperated with the stirrings of the spirit you have experienced. You have great worth, great beauty, great gifts, great holiness, and a great thirst for God. Be thankful."

I was totally drained; I sagged back on the rock, thoughts wildly racing through my head. I had spent my life looking at things one way, and now I was being challenged to look at them in a totally new way. I felt sad and raw, but also very liberated and very healed.

As I sat there, I looked down at the flat rock in time to see a raven taking one of the scraps of meat I had placed there. I jumped up and started running toward it, waving my arms. The raven flew off, and I returned to my sitting rock, disconcerted at the apparent theft.

After I regained my composure, Jesus spoke to me again. "What did you put on the rock this morning?" he asked. I was surprised, since it was very dark when I had put the meat there. Jesus had had his head lifted to the sky in prayer, and I didn't think he saw me.

"I put meat there for the animal we saw yesterday," I responded, somewhat embarrassed. "Why?" Jesus asked. "I thought it might be hungry," I said without thinking, and then I caught myself. I usually corrected an untruth in my mind before saying it, but this time, feeling that I was being grilled, I had lied. I looked at him and apologized. "That isn't the real reason," I said. "I feel led to want to connect with the animal. I don't fear him."

"Why do you want to connect with him?" Jesus asked. "I don't know," I said, "maybe it's because he seems so lonely and unloved." "Maybe it's because you're feeling so lonely and unloved," Jesus replied. "Maybe you're projecting your own unhappiness onto the animal. You realized yesterday afternoon that you're trying to attract the animal. Don't you think it's highly unusual to want to attract a potentially dangerous animal?"

I shrugged. "It's just a strong urgency in me to connect with it. I don't know where the impulse is coming from, but I'm trying to act on it. Connection with it is what I want."

"And you discovered in your ruminations yesterday afternoon that connection with me is what you want also, isn't that right?" Jesus asked. "Yes," I replied, "that is what I came back to tell you. I want a deeper connection with you, to God made present on earth." "David, you've always hungered greatly for connection with God; I honor and admire you for that hunger. You are a sincere man and not far from the kingdom of God."

Jesus continued: "Some people believe that the raven is a messenger of God, and that when the raven appears, observers should examine their hearts to discover what God is saying to them." "God has certainly spoken to me today," I said, "I am seeing things in a totally new and different light. It's exhilarating and frightening all at the same time."

"The raven needs the meat for its fledglings," Jesus added, "while your animal does not need food. Bless the raven and give it your food freely. You will be blessed in return."

I noticed that Jesus had said "your animal." Jesus read my mind and said, "It is a gift for you, something you will need far more than you realize. Why don't you go down and sit on the flat rock and see what happens. I think we've talked long enough for today."

I retrieved the two olive-wood cups and put them in my new leather carry-bag. Then I descended down the mountain a short way and sat on the flat rock. The meat scraps were all gone, and I sent a blessing with them to the raven fledglings. I sat for a long time. Jesus had given me a lot to think about. Over and over again I apologized to my father in my mind. I now saw how thoughtful he had been, in his own way, in an attempt to guide me toward the happiness and fulfillment I sought. I also saw how loving and supportive my mother had been. She had always had a special soft spot in her heart for her firstborn.

The thing I thought about most was Jesus' contention that my life was a single, linear story of God's hand in my life and of preparation for something bigger that was to come. I realized after my talk with Jesus that I had more thinking to do, more digging yet to be done. Connection with him wasn't going to be sufficient. There had to be even more.

As I sat on the flat rock, looking at Jerusalem, I was conscious of something watching me. I turned slowly and spotted the large animal standing not far behind me. It looked fierce and dangerous, but I was not afraid. "I want to be your friend," I said; "Will you be my friend?" Without hesitation, the animal came and sat down near me, just out of reach. When I started home, it walked in place by my side. I had a new companion.

MORTACI

I slowly wended my way back down the mountain. I had a lot to think about; Jesus' loving confrontation had challenged me to look at things that I had kept buried for a long time—painful things mostly having to do with my own lack of self-worth and self-love. I already felt better because of his questioning; I felt cleaner, clearer, and more focused.

I descended into the Kidron Valley, ascended the far side, and entered the gate to the city. As I walked down the dusty streets, I met acquaintances whom I had known for years. It surprised me that no one commented on the animal. I went to Aaron's shop, ostensibly to make a social call, but actually to get his reaction to my new pet. Aaron, busy with the day's activities, spent a few brief moments with me but never commented on the animal.

I left and went to Gideon's tannery, where I thanked Gideon for the leather scraps and showed him my carry-bag. I was surprised when he too didn't comment on the animal.

Finally I approached Mortaci's butcher shop. I was eager to see him, because I sensed that he might be able to explain what was going on. Mortaci was a naturalist and had a way of communing with nature and with animals. He wasn't religious per se, but he was spiritual in an unusual manner that made many people that knew him uneasy. I, however, viewed his beliefs as another entryway into the great unknown, and I sensed that he had a lot of knowledge about the natural order that few others possessed or wanted to possess.

"Well," he said when he saw me, "did the meat work to attract your animal?" "What do you think?" I asked in return. "I have no way of knowing," he said, "why don't you tell me all about it." It was now clear to me that he wasn't seeing the animal that was standing just a few feet from my side. "It turned out that I didn't need the meat to attract the animal, and a raven took it instead to feed her fledglings. The animal came to me of its own volition, and it subsequently followed me home. It's standing next to me now."

Mortaci shook his head in wonder, and then suddenly began to understand. "So you can see it right now?" he asked. "Yes," I answered, "it's visible to me all of the time." "I understand," he said, "I understand completely. I know what is going on. We all have spirits around us at all times, both good spirits and evil spirits. The Great Power of the Universe has given you an unusual and precious gift by manifesting your guardian spirit for you. I cannot see it because I have evil in my heart at the moment. My cousin has refused to pay back a significant amount of money I loaned him, and I have murderous thoughts about him. Let me try to cleanse my mind, and then see what happens."

Mortaci closed his eyes and sat very still. His breathing slowed down significantly, and he appeared to be in a stupor. I was not afraid, but rather waited patiently for his process to be over. He finally opened his eyes and said "I have forgiven my cousin and I am at peace." He looked in the direction of the animal. "I do not see the animal as you see it, but I see an aura of light, an energy field that appears to surround a very large canine." "What do you make of all of this?" I asked.

Mortaci thought for a while, and then finally spoke. "Do not be afraid," he said, "this is a great gift from the universe. Very, very few people get to see the primary energy that accompanies them through life. This is a spirit that will now accompany you and protect you. The Divine Power knows that you will need protection in the future, and that Power is showing you by this surrogate spirit that that protection will always be there for you."

He continued: "This spirit is without gender, and isn't really an animal at all. In fact, it has no physical body, so it will neither eat nor drink. It will only be visible to you until the time comes when it must become visible to others in order to protect you. Its only purpose is to attend to your well-being. You must give it a name and you must talk to it."

"I was very attracted to it from the very outset," I said, "but more for companionship and for something to love." "Like a pet," Mortaci said. "Exactly," I replied. "Well," he said, "it's not going to be quite like that. This spirit will certainly be a companion, but it will in no way be a pet." I decided to reveal the rest of the story to Mortaci. "This Jesus who I'm visiting is reputed to be the Messiah, the Son of God, and it was him who gave me this companion as a gift." I expected derision from Mortaci, but instead I got a respectful nod. "There may be something to all of this," he said; "stay with it, do not be afraid."

A sudden inspiration hit me, and I said: "I shall name this wonderful gift 'Shadow Spirit,' 'Shadow' for short. Does that seem like a good name?" "A perfect name, he said, and a perfect descriptor as well." He embraced me, and I left with Shadow to go to my shop.

On the way home, I met a neighbor who stopped me on the path. "You look different, Elder David," she said. I knew that I was getting very old, and that the morning treks to meet Jesus were fatiguing me greatly, so I expected some comment about my physical appearance. "How so?" I asked in return. She looked at me intently for quite some time. "Well," she replied, "you look more at peace, more accepting of life, and surely more connected to the rest of us, and not isolated as I have known you to be in the past."

I thanked her and continued onward, my thoughts racing. This was all new territory for me. Religion had always been a private, intellectual activity for me, totally devoid of emotions and surely devoid of supernatural events. Now I was quite possibly meeting God on a daily basis, and the list of supernatural events that had happened since my very first meeting with Jesus at his birth in Bethlehem had become extensive and quite scary.

Yes, I was afraid, and very confused as well. I had never experienced anything like this before. I sorely missed someone to talk to, someone to process things with. Oh, if only Zechariah were still alive, he would help me make sense of it all. Instead, I was the scripture scholar, the intellectual backbone of the Sanhedrin, and I was supposed to make sense out of things like this with cool, impeccable logic. But what good is logic when one meets God in person, the One who already knows everything about you?

I sat, wondering what tomorrow might bring. I hadn't seen Jesus to say good-by, so I didn't know if I would be welcome, but I decided to try to meet him in the morning.

THE CALL

I arose during the black of night. I lingered longer than usual over my morning prayers, and it seemed that I was talking to a more personal, approachable, understanding God. I again donned my everyday work tunic, placed my carry-bag over my shoulder, and left my home, navigating by starlight only. Shadow walked by my side.

When I reached the gate, the figure again stepped out of the darkness, but I was ready this time. "Shalom, Myriam" I said. I expected her to be surprised, but she wasn't. "Shalom, David," she replied, "how are you this morning?" Without answering her question, I found myself instead saying "I've thought of you often, Myriam." "And I've thought of you often as well, David." "Fondly," I added. She seemed not to hear my last remark.

"I have nourishment for the Master," she said, extending a wooden platter toward me. Before taking the dish, I reached in my carry-bag and retrieved the two wooden cups and gave them to her. "Just like Jesus," she said; "you give him one thing and get back two."

We exchanged our items but before we parted, I had something I wanted her to know, and I wasn't going to let the moment pass without saying it. "Myriam," I said, but I got no further. She gently touched my arm and cut off any further conversation by saying: "The Master is waiting and the food will get cold. You'd better go now." And with that, she slipped back into the darkness and was gone. I had failed in my attempt to tell her.

I stood in shock. When she touched me, a tremendous jolt of energy arced between us and penetrated me to my very depths. All of the repressed feelings I had been holding in erupted to the surface, feelings of loneliness, and grief for Rachel and my child, and a strong desire for a companion and a mate, and above all, a powerful need for love.

I stood under the gate and wept for a long time, crying tears that had waited decades to surface. I was deeply saddened and acutely aware of my pain. I didn't know if I could continue across the Kidron Valley and up the mountain, but I had food to deliver, so I started down the steep path, feeling my way one step at a time, with Shadow in the lead.

The journey was complicated by the fact that I had tears in my eyes most of the time. If only I had been able to successfully transmit my feelings for Myriam to her, but instead I had once again been too slow and too inexperienced to have the encounter go as I had hoped. When I reached Jesus, I was emotionally and physically drained, and sad as well.

I sat down heavily on a rock and handed Jesus the round platter. For the first time, I had enough light to see it. It was a beautiful, hand-carved piece of olive wood, with five sections around the outside and a depression in the middle in which sat a large cup. Jesus took it, raised it to heaven with both hands, praised God with thanksgiving, and blessed the food. When he lowered the platter he spread his hands apart, and once again there were two platters containing delicious food and bravitzka where moments before there had been one. He handed a platter to me, and we began to share our breakfast together.

Not wasting any time, Jesus began to question me, and again in a surprising manner. His first question came out of the blue. "How did the meeting with Myriam go?" he asked. I had already decided that, no matter what he asked, I would be totally truthful during our time together, so I responded: "Not well; I didn't manage it well and I didn't convey to her what I wanted her to know. She didn't get my message." "Oh yes she did," Jesus countered; he paused, and then continued: "It just isn't time yet for her to respond."

I didn't miss a word he said, especially the "yet" word. "Yet?", I inquired. "Yes, 'yet' " he answered and he then repeated his statement: "It just isn't time yet for her to respond." I looked at the ground, pondering his statement, but he continued his line of questioning.

"What did your friends think of Shadow?" he asked. I didn't miss the fact that he knew my spirit guardian's name without being told. "None of them could see it," I responded. "But Mortaci had some opinions about what as going on?", he continued. "Yes," I said, "Mortaci believed that the Universal Power had manifested my guardian spirit as a gift to me, but also to prepare me for what lies ahead, perhaps something dangerous. Since you told me yesterday that you had a gift for me, and then sent me down to sit on the rock, I assume that you had a hand in sending Shadow Spirit to me, and I'm grateful for that."

He changed the direction of the conversation again. "Don't be afraid, David," he said. "I know a lot is happening to you in a very short period of time, but God has favored you in a special way, and this brief time of preparation is vital and necessary."

"And painful," I added, "very painful." Jesus looked at me tenderly. "Just as the physician lances the abscess to release the pus and poison, so too we have to expose the inner psychic illnesses that would otherwise hamper you from ministering effectively."

I looked down at the ground. Jesus continued: "You had a very bad impression of your father, your father's motives, and your father's actions. And when you think of God as your father, you project your inaccurate assumptions onto God. Thus, for you, God has been a conniving, prestige-hungry power monger who doesn't really care about you and is usually emotionally absent from you. Thus, while the study of God has consumed you, you've been studying God through false premises. And further, while the study of God has been important to you, God himself hasn't been very important to you, just as your own father has not been very important to you since your earliest days."

I started crying again. It seemed like I cried more in three days than I had in all the other days of my life combined. "I have apologized to the spirit of my father over and over again in the last twenty-four hours," I whispered. "He hears you," Jesus said, "and he forgives you. Now you must forgive him as well." "I have, I do, and I will," I said. "Good," Jesus said, "so now let's put your father behind us and concentrate on God."

"What about God?", I asked. Jesus replied: "You must now ask God over and over again to forgive you, but even more importantly, you must forgive God as well. This is all very important if you are going to go to the next level." "I have, I do, and I will," I repeated.

Jesus nodded. "God your father will be a surprise to you. He is not like the Scriptures portray him; rather, he is caring, non-judgmental, forgiving, and very, very sensitive. My mission is to bring all people to the Father by showing them that He is a much different God than they have been led to believe, a much more loving God. Do you understand?"

I nodded. "Imagine what your life would have been like if you had a close, intimate relationship with your human father and also your Godly Father. What would it be like?" he asked. "It would be wonderful, fulfilling, enriching, worth everything I have," I said. "You're correct on both counts," Jesus said, "it would be worth everything you have, but it will also take everything you have to possess it. Are you willing to pay the price?"

"Yes," I responded enthusiastically, but I then immediately had the sense that I had spoken too quickly and without thinking my answer through. But Jesus seized on my "yes" and said "Well then, come follow me." Incredulous, I asked "What do you mean?" "Join me in helping to spread the good news," he replied. "How?" I asked. "That will all be shown to you. Now I am asking you to commit yourself fully to me and to my work."

I began to waffle immediately. "I am too old," I said, "too frail, too unhealthy. I have lived well past my life expectancy. I am 61 years old, and this is young men's work." I stopped talking and tried to meet Jesus' steady gaze, but eventually I looked away. "I am honored that you asked me,"

I offered, and then, hesitantly: "I will think about it and let you know. Right now, I am very, very tired, and I lack the strength to commit myself."

Jesus continued to gaze at me, saying nothing. "I get exhausted just climbing up here to meet with you," I protested, "how can I be expected to follow an itinerant Rabbi all over Judea, not to mention Galilee and elsewhere?" I stopped, realizing that my feeble protest sounded like a little child who didn't want to go to bed at bedtime. And as Jesus looked at me, I indeed felt like a little child, and a most unworthy, ungrateful one at that.

I looked over at Shadow. On the way to our meeting with Jesus, he had run ahead to greet Jesus first, and had stretched out his front legs and bowed low in greeting when he came into Jesus' presence. Now he hung in the background, head bowed, obviously devoid of the joy he had evidenced at our arrival. I had disappointed him as well.

Jesus rose. "I have to go now," he said, "the people will be looking for me." He embraced me and whispered "Shalom, David" in my ear. Maybe it was just my imagination, but it felt like his embrace was stiffer and lacked his usual enthusiasm. "Shalom, Jesus," I said, "may God go with you and richly bless your ministry."

As we separated, I noted that Jesus had tears in his eyes. He turned and walked slowly away, head bowed and shoulders hunched like a person who was sad and disappointed. "Shalom," I called again as he moved away, but I got no response in return. I dropped back down on the rock heavily, more frightened than ever. Had I also mismanaged the second encounter of the day as well? What was I supposed to have done? Why had Jesus surprised me with such a question? Couldn't he have given me more notice?

TURMOIL

Now I was alone on the mountain. I looked at the empty platters and cups. Myriam had prepared a wonderful breakfast for us: bravitzka, of course, plus warm sliced roast-lamb, warm grain patties sautéed in olive oil, cold marinated eggplant, and fresh dates. Despite my long walk up the mountain, everything was at a perfect temperature when we ate it. I looked more closely at the olive-wood cups and platters. Not only were they beautiful, but they were also spotless, like they had never been used. Not a trace of food or drink remained! Jesus at work again! It seemed like many things he did were supernatural.

Eventually I rose, put the platters and cups into my carry-bag, and wearily headed back to Jerusalem. Shadow didn't walk next to me, but rather sorrowfully dragged along behind.

I was beside myself with sadness, sorrow and, perhaps surprisingly, anger at myself as well. "Couldn't I do anything right?," I asked myself. "Now I've gone and disappointed Jesus, Myriam, and even Shadow, who's supposed to be loyal to me and my friend." My berating of myself continued: "Who was I to have wanted to meet with the Son of God? What did I want from him? And what made me think I could inter-relate with God? Or with Myriam? Or with anybody? I was a failure. Always had been a failure. Always would be a failure. A disappointment to my father, to Jesus, to everyone!"

What really bothered me was that I had continued to go deeper and deeper inside of myself, and I had finally gotten to my core need—the thing I wanted from Jesus. But I never got a chance to tell him. His line of questioning had gone in a different direction, and suddenly it was over, and just as suddenly he was gone. What I had discovered within myself was that I wanted to give love, receive love, and be of service to others from that place of love for the rest of my life. No more isolated existence for me; I wanted to share my love and God's love with everyone I encountered. But now, Jesus would never know what I had found deep within myself. Or did he know already?

I reached the Garden of Gethsemane, sat down to rest, and wept again. Shadow now sat next to me, perhaps trying to console me. I decided to spend some time making sense out of what had been a whirlwind of activity and confusion. One thing I knew for sure: Jesus was the Son of God, and I wanted to be connected with him in some fashion. This desire may have been born out of my own lonely neediness, but it was real nevertheless. My belief in Jesus had been formed in my careful dissection of the prophecies as I was guided by Zechariah, and I believed with my heart and soul that he was the Messiah.

Yet, when I was with him, I was tongue-tied, at a loss for words, a blubbering idiot. Why would he want me to come with him? And why didn't he give me some advance notice? Had he expected me to follow him that very moment? It seemed like he did. I sat in the shade and leaned against an olive tree. Questions raced through my mind, but nothing made sense. I wept off and on, until I finally sank to the moist ground and went to sleep.

THE DREAM

I fell into a deep sleep and slept for many hours, the sleep of an exhausted old man believing he was nearing the end of his life. Somewhere in the middle of my sleep, I dreamed a wonderful dream. I was a newborn, and I saw myself being carried by my father, with my smiling mother close beside. I saw the three of us approaching the temple, and I saw a middle aged man and a slightly older woman coming to greet us.

"What have we here?" Simeon said. "My firstborn son," my beaming father replied; "we have come to have him blessed, and to consecrate him to God." Simeon responded: "I take you at your word. You must give him up and allow him to follow the Lord. He will be the old, wise one for the Lord just as I am. He will never make a good merchant!"

"How do you know I'm a merchant?" my father asked. "I see things others don't see," responded Simeon, "and I see this son of yours not blossoming until very late in life. Until then, he will be a disappointment for you, and you will pass on before you see his value, but I promise you, the Lord will use him in a powerful manner before he dies."

My father lowered his eyes, but raised them again when Anna began to speak. "This boy of yours has been chosen for a special role in salvation history. He will struggle through life, but that struggle will lead him to the truth, and the truth will empower him to be a guide for many younger men who will benefit from his learning and his life experience."

"What do you intend to name him?" asked Simeon. "Jacob," my mother said, "the same as his father." Anna was obviously filled with the Spirit, and she spoke again: "The boy should be named 'David'," she said, "because he is especially chosen by God to make God's kingdom great, just as King David did." My parents both gasped. At that time, no one named a child "David," because it was considered presumptuous and arrogant to assume that any child could match the deeds of Israel's great ancestor-king.

Simeon added: "Name him David, and lest you think that our suggestion is ill-founded, you should know that no one will ever question your judgment about this. Watch and see; people will just take it for granted that you had reason for naming him as you have."

"Let's find the priest of the day to bless this wonderful child," said Simeon. "Can Anna and I accompany you? This is a special child, and we want to be part of the blessing."

"Ah, here comes Zechariah. He is a wonderful new priest who is a holy man and who doesn't rush through consecrations to get his stipend. This is a blessing that it's him."

After introducing himself, Zechariah lifted me high above his head and prophesied that this was a special day in salvation history, and that I had been chosen to assist God in the salvation of many people. "And what will he be called?", Zechariah asked. My parents exchanged glances, and then it was my mother who spoke: "He shall be called 'David,' for he will help save God's people, Israel. Praise be to Yahweh. Yes, praise be to him."

INSPIRATION

I awoke after many hours. The sun was high in the sky, and it had gotten quite warm. A small trickle of water ran down the side of a moss-covered stone wall on the border of the garden, and I walked there and drank deeply of the cool, spring-fed water for a long time.

I felt refreshed, and no longer remorseful about the day's events. The dream had been a great enlightenment, and I now knew what I had to do, and what I wanted to do. I was reenergized from the sleep and from the water, and I immediately started down the east side of the Kidron Valley. Shadow had perked up too, and he once again walked by my side. We crossed the valley, ascended its west side, and entered the East Gate of the city.

I went straight to my shop. Two pairs of half-finished sandals sat on my workbench, one pair for Mortaci and one pair for me. I worked efficiently and had them completed by mid-afternoon. "What brings you here?" Mortaci asked as I appeared in his shop door, "you seem out of breath." "I've been hurrying, to finish and deliver your new sandals." I said. "Here they are." "They're beautiful as always," Mortaci noted, "but what's this about hurrying?" I paused for a moment, but I knew that Mortaci might be the only person to affirm me in what I was setting out to do, so I responded: "I'm leaving in the morning to go with Jesus, and I may be gone for an extended period of time." He came around his butcher table to embrace me: "Bless you, David, the Lord be with you. And be sure to take Shadow, because you will need his guidance and protection in the future."

PREPARATION

I returned to my shop, wrapped most of my tools in an old tunic, and went next-door to my neighbor's house. After greeting one another, I said to him: "I am going away for an extended period of time. Can I ask you to watch over my tools?" He nodded. "Come with me," he said. He took me to the back wall of his small bedroom, and carefully removed a stone from the wall. Behind the stone was concealed a small hiding place, and he placed the tools inside, next to a small bag of coins and some jewelry hidden there. "If I am not here when you return," he said, "your tools will still be safely hidden here."

By now it was late afternoon. I placed my new, spare pair of sandals, my elder's cloak, a few leather-working tools, and a prayer shawl in my carry-bag along with the platters and cups already packed there. I moved my work bench and outside furniture to the inside of my house, and I shuttered the windows and doors for the first time since I had lived there.

With my preparations complete, I was moved to walk to the temple, where I sat in quiet reflection until dusk. As I returned I passed Mortaci's house, and spotting me, he cried out: "Come in and break bread with me for the last time for awhile. My wife has cooked some goat meat, and I have cheese, some fresh fruit, home-made bread, and good wine. You will need the nourishment for your journey and your new adventures. Come, come."

After the second delicious meal of the day, I thanked Mortaci and his wife and returned home, where I sat with one lit candle, praying and thinking about the coming new day.

DESOLATION AND DESPAIR

I slept fitfully, awaking often with thoughts of the new day and my new adventure. My life seemed to finally have purpose, and I was about to receive what I had always wanted: connection with God and a viable way to serve Him. I was full of joyous expectation.

Unable to sleep any more, I arose and re-lit my candle, and sat praying about my new life. I saw the candle as a metaphor for Jesus: one lone flame, lighting up the universe. I prayed earnestly that I would be able to serve in whatever way Jesus wanted me to.

I was so full of anticipation that finally I could wait no longer, so I slung the carry-bag over my shoulder and started out, Shadow by my side. When I reached the East Gate, I should have immediately known that something was wrong, because Myriam was not there with her offering of bravitzka and food. I even called her name several times into the darkness, but there was no answer. Myriam had not appeared. I wondered why, but pressed on.

Outside the gate, Shadow ran ahead and proceeded up the north path along the wall of the temple. I wondered how my guardian could have gotten confused about the direction in which we were going. Up until this moment, I had not spoken to him, so I didn't know what to do. Does one speak to a Spirit, and if so, can the Spirit be expected to answer?

Instead, I continued onto the path across the Kidron Valley, and eventually Shadow reluctantly joined me, lagging behind and seemingly very unhappy about my decision.

As I pressed on across the valley and up the steep far side I thought about my relationship with Shadow, or more precisely, my lack of relationship with him. I had put out water and food for him for a few days, but as Mortaci had predicted, Shadow touched neither. Shadow seemed to communicate with me solely by body language, and at the moment, he was showing me that he had little interest in climbing the Mount of Olives. This was surprising, because on the previous morning, he had run ahead, eager to meet Jesus.

I continued the exhausting ascent and finally came to the meeting spot. I was appalled to discover that Jesus was not there. "Maybe I'm too early," I thought hopefully, "after all, it is still dark." But deep within, I knew better. Jesus had not committed to meet me on this fourth morning, and now Shadow's reluctance and Myriam's absence all made sense.

I looked around, calling out Jesus' name, but in vain. I looked at the terrain; this indeed was a desolate spot, and I suddenly realized that it was Jesus' presence and his aura that made it special; without him, it was just arid wilderness, full of rocks and thorn bushes.

I sat on my rock, and the enormity of my missed opportunity swept over me. The Son of God had asked me to come with him, and I had temporized so as to complete my own petty agenda. I realized that in the three days of encounters, I was mostly full of myself and my own needs, rather than absorbing Jesus' words fully and trying to discern what God wanted from me. I sat on the rock and began to weep again. As an adult I had never cried, and now it seemed that that was all I was doing. I sat on the rock and despaired.

SPIRIT GUIDANCE

I wept bitterly for a long time, feeling that my life was now empty and truly over. Shadow sat and watched me for a respectable time. I was finally conscious of his gaze. Up until now, he was just something that followed me around, a true shadow for me. We didn't yet have a relationship and I didn't understand why Jesus provided him for me.

I sat looking at him through my tears, trying to decide what to do next. I saw no other option except to trudge back down the mountain and return to my leather-working shop. "What would Mortaci and my neighbors say when I returned unsuccessful and unhappy?" I thought. "What had happened to my grand ambition to serve this Jesus?" I would be embarrassed, a daft old man who thought he could accompany the Son of God! Surely, the whole city would eventually hear about my futile attempt to answer his call.

I faced Shadow again. I now realized that he had been trying to guide me to go north that morning, but I had single-mindedly and blindly pressed on across the Kidron Valley and up the mountain, ignoring the direction that Shadow was providing and ignoring Myriam's absence as well. The signs had been there to enlighten me, but I ignored them.

I looked at Shadow and began talking to him. "I am starting to understand your role in my life," I said, "and from now on, as far as I am able, I will trust your guidance and direction. Please help me now to find Jesus if it be God's will to do so. Please, please."

PURSUIT

Shadow arose and briskly started to walk in a different direction from the path by which we had arrived. I was exhausted and full of sadness, but I decided to follow Shadow to the best of my ability, wherever he led me. However, when I stood up, doubts began to overtake me immediately, because Shadow was proceeding through an apparently impassable area of wilderness, full of strewn boulders, briars, thistles and ravines.

Then I remembered my pledge to trust Shadow's guidance and direction, and I started out to follow him. After a while, I realized that he was heading north on a small game trail that was almost imperceptible to the casual observer. We wended our way between the various hazards, and I discovered that the path was easier to traverse than I had imagined.

After a few hours, the sun had risen high into the sky, and it had gotten very hot. I was unused to so much exercise, and the physical and emotional drain of the last three days were taking their toll on me. I began to falter, and I wasn't sure I could continue. About then, Shadow left the path and went about twenty paces into the boulders. I followed and found a little spring flowing out of the rock. I realized that I had not had anything to drink yet that day, and I was dehydrated. I retrieved a bravitzka cup from my carry-bag and knelt down to fill it with water. As I did, I saw a glint at the bottom of the little pool.

I reached into the water and withdrew a beautiful gemstone, and I was moved to drop it into my empty coin bag. I drank deeply from the spring, and refreshed, I continued on.

THE SIGHTING

I had splashed the spring water over my head for an extended period of time, and the bodily hydration combined with a newfound sense of hope engendered by Shadow's confident demeanor gave me renewed energy and stamina. We continued north through arid wilderness, and I somehow drew on inner resources of stamina to keep going. Shadow's pace indicated we had catching up to do, and I managed to keep up with him.

Late in the morning, we crested the last of the several small mountains we had traversed, and I gazed down at the arid plain below us. In the far distance, I saw a small band of men heading north, and by Shadow's increased pace, I sensed that the band consisted of Jesus and His followers. Shadow led me to another cool spring where I drank deeply and also splashed myself with water, and thus renewed, we continued in pursuit of the band.

Being over 60 years of age, I had a self-image of myself as old, frail and feeble, so I was surprised that I was able to keep going. "Could it be that God is energizing me so that I can connect with Jesus and begin to serve him?" I asked myself. We descended quickly to the desert floor and began walking rapidly to close ground on the band in the distance. The men seemed to be casually strolling along, talking, and I was heartened when the distance between us began to shrink noticeably. Shadow now walked a small distance ahead of me, and often turned and looked at me as if to offer encouragement and support. When the band of men stopped at a shaded well to rest, I knew we would overtake them.

THE ENCOUNTER

Despite the refreshing water at the two springs, fatigue started to overtake me. I had not eaten since the night before at Mortaci's, and I knew my energy reserves were giving out. Only the fact that the men ahead were sitting down for their noon-day rest kept me going.

As we finally drew near, I realized that I didn't know what I was going to say to Jesus; I had been so intent on catching up to him that I hadn't thought about rehearsing anything. While we were yet a short distance away, Jesus spotted us, arose, and walked a short distance back along the path we were on and then stopped. I was relieved to find that it was indeed him. I expected him to continue toward us; upon meeting, I expected an exchange of the kiss of peace and the greeting of "Shalom," but I was badly mistaken.

Jesus stood in the path, gazing at me, and I suddenly felt powerless and very unfit for any kind of service for him. Additionally, I felt shame about having not responded promptly on the previous morning, and if the truth be known, I felt very inadequate and unworthy.

I was surprised by what happened next. I collapsed on the ground in exhaustion, and all of my pain, turmoil, frustration and self-doubt began pouring out in a torrent of tears. I could not speak, and I sobbed uncontrollably. I laid there for a long time. I expected Jesus to approach me, console me, and help me to my feet, but such was not the case. Instead, he left me lying there in the dust and camel dung, sobbing in pain and despair.

I sobbed for a long time, almost hyperventilating as the deep pain of my self-perceived wasted life washed over me. I sobbed until there was no more left to come out, until I was empty and totally vulnerable. Jesus stood about ten paces away, silently watching me. I finally regained some measure of composure and looked up, my clothes and beard streaked with tears mixed with dirt and animal droppings. I somehow met Jesus' gaze, and I whispered "I'm sorry" over and over again. "Sorry for what?", he challenged.

"For disappointing you, for not saying 'Yes' to you immediately when you invited me to follow you yesterday, for a life of emptiness and loneliness, for my sinfulness, for never measuring up to what others thought I could be, for everything that now saddens me."

Jesus responded: "Do you remember our talk about everything that has happened to you thus far being a preparation for service?" I nodded my head. "It was necessary that you see and touch all of the pain and misery within you, and sob it out onto the path. It was necessary that you realize that you cannot serve me out of your own strength. You are empty now, and clean" he said, "and fully prepared to serve, fully prepared to do what you were born to do, and what only you can do. Are you ready for this discipleship? If so, then come now and follow me, and I will give you the strength to persevere."

"I am not worthy," I said, looking back at the ground. He continued to gaze at me, waiting. I could think of nothing else to say, so I repeated "I am not worthy," but then more words came to my lips, and I added "but only say the word, and I shall be healed."

"I say the word," Jesus responded, "you are healed and you are worthy, and you will accomplish great things in my name, and with my support and blessing. Now come, the others are waiting." I started to crawl toward him, but as his words sunk in, I realized that I no longer had to crawl so I arose. Jesus did not close the distance by approaching me, but rather allowed me to walk the whole way to him. I opened my arms to embrace him in thanksgiving, and he returned the embrace warmly, whispering "Welcome, and Shalom" in my ear. I drew back, afraid that my badly soiled garments had dirtied his white tunic, but I was amazed to find that both his clothes and mine were totally clean.

"Before we join the others," I said, "I want you to know that I have finally recognized what I want. I want to love, to be loved, and to serve others humbly from that place of love." "Like Myriam serves," he said, once again catching me off guard. "Yes, like Myriam serves," I said sadly. "Don't be sad about her," he said, "your time will come."

He now took my arm to support me; I hadn't realized how weak and shaky I had gotten. We walked onward to the small band of men resting in the shade. I was surprised at how young they all were, and also how crude and unpolished they all seemed. "This is David, our newest member," Jesus said; "Do we have some food and drink left that he might have for his mid-day repast?" The younger men scurried about and produced dried fish, bread and dates from their various tote bags, and a cup of cold water was handed to me as well. Jesus introduced me to each man and gave a brief profile of each, after which the men resumed the small talk among themselves as if a new member was nothing unusual.

THE COMMISSIONING

As soon as I had finished eating, the men rose and continued their travel northward on the road. Jesus helped me to my feet, and we walked together several paces behind the others. Both Jesus and I knew that this ministry would be physically rigorous for anyone, and especially for me at my advanced age and with my various ailments and frailties.

"I have some things about which to talk to you," I said to Jesus. He nodded. "First, thank you for Shadow. I greatly appreciate this special gift." Jesus surprised me again, as if reading my mind. "You can talk to Shadow, praise him, thank him, express your love for him, and ask him for what you need. He was given to you as a helpmate, and you will need his help far more than you realize. Just another part of your preparation."

I reached in my hidden pouch and produced the gemstone. "Thanks to Shadow, I found this magnificent stone. I don't know if it's worth anything, but it reminds me of the beauty of God's creation, and I want you to have it to help support your ministry." Jesus smiled and said: "Thank you, David. I accept it but I want you to carry it in your coin pouch and tell no one about it. I will direct you on how it is to be used at a later time."

"One more question," I said. Jesus laughed out loud, knowing that I never had only "one more question." "What exactly do you want me to do? I don't have any idea about how I can assist you, and frankly, I feel very ill-equipped for this ministry. But I trust you."

Jesus smiled again, and then got very serious. "David, there are no accidents, and life isn't a random series of events with no meaning and no inter-connectedness. As I have said before, everything that you've experienced has been preparation for this day and this ministry. Back on the road I let you lie in the dirt and sob out the last of your hurts and disappointments so you would be fully emptied and fully ready for this spiritual journey. From the day of your consecration to God by Zechariah until now, you've been chosen."

"I felt so unworthy and so unprepared," I said, "and I still do, but not in a debilitating way like before. I wondered why you didn't come to me and console me when I was in such pain on the road, but now I understand. Forgive me for being a bit slow to grasp things. I'm new to being in personal relationship with God and I don't know how to act."

"God?" Jesus asked. "Yes, Jesus, I believe that you are the Son of God and the Messiah." Ever conscious about telling the entire truth, I continued: "Sometimes a wave of doubt washes over me, but behind and beneath the doubt is the firm certainty that you are the Chosen One who will redeem the world." He nodded. "If only you knew how much I value and love you, David" he said, "you would dance in this road. Your faith is wonderful to behold, and your sincerity is without question. You have always been a man of God, but your past wounds kept you from seeing how close you are to God."

He continued: "You are the only man I would consider for the work I have for you to do. You will be the foundation on which I build up this band of men. I really need you."

I was in shock. "The foundation?" I asked. "Yes," Jesus responded. "We are going to Galilee, where I will work among the people for an extended period of time, as the men I have chosen get to know me and one another. But later, my effort will mostly center around preparing them to carry on my work throughout Israel and later the world. By the time the preparation period arrives, you will have earned their admiration and respect and you will play a critical role in preparing these men for their mission. It won't be easy."

"I don't know how to do this," I said candidly, "I have always been a loner, content to work my leather and study Scripture. I'm not good at inter-personal relationships." "One thing you must continually keep in mind," Jesus said, "I believe in you and I have chosen you. My strength I give you will be sufficient for the rigors of the journey, and My Spirit will instruct you on how to serve me and how to serve those men. They need you badly."

I was hanging on every word Jesus spoke. "Tell me how to act," I said. Jesus smiled and touched my shoulder. "That is the simplest thing of all," he said laughingly, "just be yourself." He continued: "Let me make it as clear as possible. These men need a grandfather, a wise man who has experienced life to the fullest and who has a perspective on God and the world that can be shared. These men will experience the gamut of emotions, from sadness to anger to joy to fear. They will need a keel in their lives, someone who is steady and who keeps the boat afloat and headed in the right direction. They will have doubts, and they will have questions they'll be afraid to ask me. That's where you come in. You'll be the approachable, invaluable constant in the group."

I responded: "I hereby give up all my doubts and uncertainties, all of my limiting self-beliefs. Since you have called me and believe in me and believe that I am capable of doing your will, I will trust that I will be up to the task. I'm honored to be chosen."

We walked on in silence for a while. Then Jesus said: "I am going ahead to rejoin the group. I'm sure you could use some quiet time alone to process all that we've discussed. Don't worry about walking back here alone because we'll never leave you behind again."

I touched His arm. "Thank you," I said, "thank you for all that you have given me. It's like having a new and challenging life to live, just when I thought I was ready to die." Jesus patted my hand and smiled, saying "It's a new adventure that we'll share together."

I trudged along by myself, reflecting on all that had happened. It seemed impossible that my first meeting with Jesus was just four days ago. It felt like more had happened to me in those four days than in the remainder of my life altogether. My mind was in turmoil, with conflicting thoughts and questions racing through it. Would I ever see my home and my shop again? Would I dine with Mortaci in the future? And what about Myriam; would I ever see her again? And most significantly, how was I supposed to act now?

"Jesus had indicated that it was okay for me to walk apart and behind the group. Was that always to be the case? Wasn't such behavior anti-social, even unfriendly? How was I to answer the doubts that his disciples had?" The questions raged through my mind.

PHILIP

One of the men left the group ahead of me, stopped by the side of the path and waited for me to reach him. "May I join you?" he said. "Certainly," I responded. "Are you sure?" he inquired, "I don't want to disturb you." "No, you're not disturbing me," I answered with a smile. "In fact, some company would be welcome. I'm lonely. Please join me."

"My name is Philip," he offered, "and I want to welcome you to our little band." "Why thank you," I replied, "you are the first to reach out to me." He nodded. "How long have you been with Jesus?" I asked. "A few weeks," he responded, "I was one of the first to be asked, or more precisely, to be called forth." "How did it happen?" I asked.

"Jesus first appeared at the Jordan River, where John the Baptist was preaching and baptizing. The same day, I had gone to the Jordan River to hear John, who called us to repent, leave behind our sinful ways, and prepare for the coming of God's kingdom. His words seemed to be aimed directly at me. I was baptized with the other folks, and it touched my soul beyond measure. I resolved to change my lifestyle." Philip paused, looked at me, and decided to continue. "Jesus was baptized last that day," he said, "and it was a very moving experience for me." "Did you hear the voice?" I said. Philip looked startled and surprised. "How did you know about that?" he asked. "I was there in the crowd," I responded. Philip seemed relieved. "Yes, some of us heard the voice and saw the dove, although some others in the crowd did not," he said. "It was very powerful."

"Every one of us was profoundly moved," Philip continued. "I recognized that Jesus was a different kind of person. I wanted to meet him but didn't. He immediately disappeared without a trace for a lengthy period of time. When he reappeared, it's my understanding that he came out of the wilderness east of the Sea of Galilee," Phillip said. "Those who saw him at that time reported that he was physically weak and malnourished, and yet he exuded strength and self-confidence and resolve. He had an irresistible aura of holiness, serenity and presence. When he looked at you, it was like he could see your soul."

"He first invited Simon and Andrew to join him, and they immediately put down their nets and walked away from their life-time livelihood. The same was true of James and John—John, who is still an adolescent. Next he called me, and I brought Nathaniel with me. Nathaniel recognized and acknowledged that Jesus was the Son of God during the first few moments of their meeting. Jesus traveled to Bethsaida, where I live, and then headed southward toward Judea, calling more members with no apparent rhyme or reason. We're surely a diverse group, and none of us yet know what we are getting into."

"Why did you join him?" I asked. "My father is wealthy," he replied. "I have never had to work, so I became lazy and self-indulgent. My father became very critical of me, and the friction between us intensified. One day, in a fit of anger, my father threatened to disown me and evict me from his home unless I began doing something productive with my life. Meanwhile, my father invited Jesus to our home. When Jesus came to dine at our house with his first followers, he took me aside and invited me to join the group."

"I saw it as a way out of my contentious relationship with my father, and it appeared that it was going to be an easy life without too much effort involved. Since my father liked Jesus, I suspected that he'd approve of my decision."

"It sounded like an adventure," he continued, "and I was pretty naïve about what it would entail. Now I realize that I have enlisted for more than I bargained for, and that this experience might involve more than I am capable of doing." "Why do you say that?" I queried. "This mission, if I can call it that, calls for holy, dedicated men," he responded, "and I am certainly not holy. Nor was I dedicated," he continued, "until I was baptized and was called to join the group. Since then, I have had time to think. I'm afraid I'm in over my head. I'm deeply concerned." "I feel the same way," I answered, "but I trust that Jesus knows what he is doing, and he believes we are up to the task."

Philip went on: "When we got to Bethany, Jesus rested several days there, praying and regaining his strength and vitality. That's when he met you." Philip continued: "There are already lots of rumors in Jerusalem about him. Some people are afraid of him, others are excited about his presence, but most are just curious and want to see him themselves."

"Why did you join?" Phillip asked, staring directly into my eyes. I replied: "Ever since my new wife and our baby died during childbirth, I have lived an isolated life, working in my shop and studying Scripture by myself. Jesus helped me see that I had equated loving with being hurt, and that I had been grieving all these years, instead of moving forward. I finally realized that I want to love and be loved, and that I want to serve others lovingly."

THE CONVERSION

Philip and I continued conversing well into the afternoon. Shortly before dusk, the group reached a small village of five or six small, stone huts, located in the middle of a stony, arid area. Jesus approached the nearest house, where a small girl was playing in the dirt. She ran into the house, frightened, when we all appeared. A balding man then appeared in the doorway. He looked tired and old before his time. He scowled at us.

"What do you want?" he said. "We need food and a place to spend the night," Jesus replied. "We have no food, and this certainly isn't an inn," he said. "There's a larger village further down the road," he continued; "you might find what you need there."

The small girl came back out of the hovel and walked a short distance down the road, where she commenced to sit in the dirt again. She had an ugly sore on her face, which was obviously very infected, and black and blue marks appeared on her arms and legs.

"What happened to your daughter?" Jesus asked. "She took a bad fall among the rocks," the man lied, "and we cannot afford a doctor or medicine that might help her." Jesus gazed into the man's eyes and quietly said: "You beat her with your walking stick." The man opened his mouth, prepared to deny the fact, but thought better of it, and looking down at the ground, muttered: "She was bad, and deserved it. Maybe I pounded some sense into her head." He looked back up from the ground, facing Jesus defiantly.

Jesus addressed him again. "Children that young aren't bad. She did nothing deserving of the terrible beating you gave her. Your father beat you and abandoned you, and you are now passing on your lifetime of anger and resentment by heaping the same very painful abuse on your daughter."

The man scuffed his feet in the dirt. "You'd better move on now," he said, "we aren't going to be able to help you." "Do you mind if I talk to your daughter?" Jesus asked politely. "Take her with you," the man replied, "for otherwise she will surely starve here with the rest of us." A voice from inside let out a wail: "No, never; do not take my daughter," said the mother, appearing in the doorway. "We will find a way to survive."

Jesus nodded toward the road, indicating that we should all continue on out of the small village. I looked back after a few hundred paces, and I saw Jesus kneeling in the dirt, talking to the child. As I watched, she got up and crept into his arms, and I watched him hold her tenderly for a long while. Her parents were also watching from their doorway. After an extended period, she ran back to the hovel, while Jesus rejoined us on the road.

A few minutes later, we heard a shout and turned to discover that the man was now running up the road toward us. When he reached us, I saw that he had a small loaf of bread in his hands. "Who are you?" he asked Jesus. "I am Jesus of Nazareth," Jesus replied. "How did you heal my daughter so completely?" the man asked. "Love can heal many wounds," Jesus said, "and I love your daughter like your Father loves you." "My father beat me daily," the man said, "and he never once showed any love for me."

"I speak of your Father in heaven," Jesus said. "He loves you unconditionally." "You had better leave me now," the man said, "for I am a sinful man. But take this with you for your journey." The man extended his hand, offering the small loaf of bread to Jesus.

"That is all the food you have, isn't it?" Jesus asked. At first the man thought that Jesus was being ungrateful, but after looking at Jesus' face, he simply responded "Yes it is, but there's our abandoned orchard a bit further down the road. There's a fresh spring there, and perhaps you can find a few pieces of dried-up fruit hanging on the branches or laying on the ground. You can sleep there as well," the man continued quietly.

Jesus looked at the man and asked: "Why have you abandoned the orchard?" "It no longer bears fruit," the man responded. "It no longer bears fruit because you no longer tend it," Jesus replied. "How do you know?", the man asked, "have you seen it already?" "I know because you are bitter and have stopped trying," Jesus responded. "You are hopeless and are just waiting to die so you can escape from your wretched existence." "You read my heart," the man said, and turning, he prepared to leave, forgetting to give the bread in has hand to Jesus. "Do you want the bread of life?" Jesus said to his back.

The man turned back. "You mean this meager little loaf?" he asked. "No," Jesus responded, "I mean bread that will let you live forever." The man frowned. "We are starving" he said, "and you are making light of our situation.

You'd better leave now." "What would it be worth if I promised you eternal life?" Jesus asked.

The man thought for a while. "You mean you can show me how to live forever?" he asked. "Your body may die, but your spirit will live forever if you listen to me," Jesus said. "Your wife and daughter and friends—yes, the whole world, can live forever too."

"What must I do?" the man asked. "Pray to your Father in heaven morning and night," Jesus replied. "Think of Him frequently during the day. Love your wife and daughter, and be good to them. Forgive your enemies, and welcome the stranger who comes to your door. Work hard: prune your orchard, plant vegetable seeds between the trees, and plant grain in the fields around the little spring. Approach your Father with love and hope, and ask Him for your daily sustenance and for forgiveness for your past mistakes."

The man fell to his knees and embraced Jesus' feet. "I don't know how to pray," he said, "I've never been taught how to pray. Teach me how to pray." Jesus responded: "Here is how to pray to your heavenly Father: 'Dear Father, who loves me faithfully and all of the time despite my weaknesses, show me how to live. Bless my labors. Help me love my family. Remove my shame and guilt, and let me praise you with a clean heart'."

"Thank you, Master, I can pray like that," the man said. Standing up, he again offered the bread to Jesus. Jesus took the small loaf, looked to heaven as he blessed it, broke it in half, and returned half to the man. "Each day, eat half of what I am returning to you," Jesus said, and leave the rest for the morrow. You will not starve if you obey my words. Remember, your Father in heaven loves you just as I have loved you. Now go in peace."

DUSK

We left the peaceful, now-blessed man and continued on to the orchard. It was badly overgrown, and hardly any fruit was visible. Reality was sinking in: this was to be a hard life, with truly primitive conditions devoid of comfortable amenities. No latrines, no straw mat to sleep on, and no warm blankets. A bit of begged food, and not much more.

I watched as a quiet little man named Judas, son of James, apparently took control of the preparation of the evening meal. He humbly assigned a task to each man in the group: one to fill a gourd half-full of water, another to find a handful of olives, others to look for abandoned fruit, others to find firewood, and still others to clear a place for us to recline.

Judas took a small metal pan from his tote-bag, and when the first man returned with a few olives, Judas crushed them and covered the bottom of the pan with the olive oil he had produced. Next he broke the bread into tiny crumbs and spread it around in the pan, allowing it to mix with the olive oil so that he could produce a doughy substance. When other men returned with a few pieces of fruit, Judas mashed them with a rounded stone, catching the juice in the gourd half-full of water, and placing the remaining mush into the dough-lined pan. Finally, he took the dates another man had found, cut them into small, bite-sized pieces with a stone knife, and stirred them into the fruity mixture in the bowl.

While all of this was occurring, Jesus withdrew and was seen praying in a quiet place, as was his custom. I remained seated in the shade, totally spent from the day's exertion.

Bartholomew had an important responsibility: carrying a live spark in tinder inside a small, pottery container made for the purpose. He now used the spark to start a fire. When the dead wood had burned down to coals, Judas hung his metal pan above them, close enough for the pan to absorb the heat, but not so close that the meal would be scorched. Soon, a wondrous aroma drifted up from the concoction, and I began to salivate in anticipation of the meal.

Jesus returned from his prayer time, and when Judas deemed the meal ready, Jesus used damp grass to grasp the hot metal pan in one hand, so as not to burn himself, and then held the gourd of fruit punch in the other. He raised the food and drink above his head, thanked the Father for the meal, blessed it, and set it back down on a flat rock. I had had very little to eat in several days, and I was so hungry that I believed I could eat the whole meal. Even with small portions, I estimated the pan of food would only feed four men at most.

Jesus again picked up the pan and, out of respect for my age, approached to serve me first. I quickly retrieved one of the olive-wood cups and plates from my carry-bag. Using a wooden spoon, Jesus placed a sizable portion on my plate, and Judas followed with the small gourd of fruit punch, filling my cup to the top. I started to protest that they had given me too much, but Jesus smiled and touched my arm in a reassuring manner.

I watched in amazement as Jesus fed the entire group from the small pan and Judas gave everyone a generous portion of the fruity drink, and I was even more amazed when Jesus placed the metal pan back above the coals and I could see that it still remained half-full. The meal was delicious, and many of us took a second helping when Jesus offered it.

During the serving, I noticed that Judas Iscariot had no plate or cup. He had seemed to avoid me since I joined the group earlier in the day, but I had resolved to serve out of love, so I decided to make a generous gesture to him. Judas had eaten his meal off a flat stone he had found, and he rudely repeatedly quaffed the drink directly from the gourd.

Consequently, I approached him after the meal and offered him my spare olive-wood plate and cup, which he accepted with no more than a grunt of acknowledgement. I walked away, hoping that my relationship with him would improve as time went on.

After the meal, the men disrobed and took turns bathing themselves as best they could under the small spring that sprang out of the rocks and fell onto the ground, forming a small pool. More dead-fall was added to the fire, and the men sat naked around it, drying themselves and their clothes and making small talk about the day's adventures.

I was exhausted, and after washing I found a quiet place with thick green grass covering the ground. I stretched out and looked up at the stars. It seemed years ago that I had left my leather-working shop to go up the mountain to meet Jesus, only to find him gone, but instead I realized that it had been earlier on this very day. So much had happened, I was overwhelmed as I thought about the day's events. Would every day be this full, I wondered, or would I experience a less demanding pace as I acclimated to this life? I wondered if I had behaved as Jesus wanted me to, and I wondered further what would be asked of me in the future. I whispered a prayer for strength, and then drifted off to sleep.

BETRAYAL

My amazement continued the next morning. Bartholomew stirred the coals and got the fire going again, and Judas put the metal pan containing a few scraps of the previous night's meal over the fire. The gourd was refilled with water, and we then said our morning prayers. Jesus again offered the food and drink up in blessing, and we commenced to eat.

Jesus served the food, Judas, son of James served the drink, and everyone again was fully satisfied. I noticed that Judas Iscariot again ate off of the flat stone and drank directly from the gourd, but I remained silent. We broke camp and started again on the road north. I wondered if the man and his family had followed Jesus' instructions and only ate a portion of the bread, and if they would keep faith with what Jesus had bid them to do.

I walked all day alone, a few paces behind the group. I liked being alone, especially on a day like this when I had so much to think about, so much to absorb. By noon it was very hot, and the group took cover at a shaded oasis. Judas Iscariot procured some dried fruit for lunch, and also obtained some fresh vegetables and salted fish for the evening meal.

We rested in the shade during the heat of the day and then later resumed walking until sunset. The evening was much like the previous one. Despite my protestations I was respectfully told that I should rest in the shade while the others prepared the meal. Our cook again directed everyone as to what was needed, and then produced a tasty meal.

Jesus said the blessing and then proceeded to give each of us a generous portion of food and drink, starting again with me. The dried fish and fresh vegetables had been blended into a delicious fish stew, and the water was again flavored with fruit juice.

Once again, Judas Iscariot failed to use the olive-wood set I had given him, and I could no longer keep myself from inquiring about it. When asked, Judas replied: "Why, I sold the set to a merchant in the last village." "You sold the set to a merchant?" I asked in stunned disbelief. "Yes, I did," he said defiantly, "and I got a handsome price for it too."

I turned away in shock. Myriam had sent the first beautiful set to Jesus containing food and drink, and Jesus had cloned it into a second set for me as he said the blessing. How could Judas have taken such a priceless gift and sold it to a nameless stranger? I wanted to return to the last village and buy it back, but I realized I had no money. The set was surely gone forever, and I felt like I had disappointed Myriam and Jesus by giving it up.

I looked at Judas again. He was smirking with self-satisfaction. I felt hatred for him run through my body; all of my dealings with him had been like this, and I resented that fact.

I walked away and sat down on a stone. I knew what Jesus would advise me to do, but it was very hard to forgive such a callous, insensitive person. And his smug demeanor when found out made my negative feelings for him even stronger. I prayed, and I finally forgave him as much as I could at that moment, but I realized I had more forgiving to do.

ANDREW

The next morning broke cloudy and chilly, and I was glad I had brought a warm cloak along. After breakfast we headed northward at a leisurely pace. I walked behind, alone. Until now, Philip was the only one to have walked with me, but Jesus hadn't given me further direction after telling me to "be yourself," so I was content bringing up the rear.

I spent the morning wondering about the men Jesus had chosen, and what they thought about Jesus. Surely they had observed his miracles, such as healing the little girl and multiplying our food on several occasions, or had they? Perhaps they just took it for granted, I thought, without realizing the supernatural quality of what he was doing.

I thought about Judas Iscariot too, and my need to forgive him more than I had. I came to the realization that his behavior was motivated by his past experiences which I neither knew nor understood, and while his actions were unacceptable to me, they were what he felt he had to do. I couldn't see his heart so I shouldn't judge his actions, no matter how distasteful they were to me. He was who he was, and I would have to deal with that fact.

I realized too that my deep hurt about the olive-wood set was because Myriam had sent the first set along to Jesus, and Jesus had turned one set into two. I was looking forward to returning both sets to her, and seeing her again. I wanted to find a way to let her know how fond I was of her, and to be in her presence longer than a few moments at daybreak.

Then another realization hit me: it wasn't the monetary value of the olive-wood set that had upset me so deeply, but rather the emotional value of the items, and after all, I still had the emotional memories to cling to. Myriam was now a part of me, whether or not I had a memento of hers in my tote bag. For me, she was the embodiment of truly loving service, and I intended to learn from her thoughtfulness and share such love with others.

Then I thought of fathers: my father, Philip's father, Mortaci's father, Zechariah, and all the other fathers I had known. I realized that it was difficult to be a father, and that often, despite a man's best intentions, his son ended up disappointing him by not measuring up to his standards. The sons recognized this and thereby unconsciously sabotaged their father's plan for them, and the ensuing hurt and friction drove a wedge between them that oftentimes never got healed and resolved. Yes, being a father was a difficult assignment.

Jesus often referred to God as his father and our father, so I wondered about God as well. Surely He must be disappointed in our failure to measure up to all that He hoped we would be and do, and I wondered if His disappointment would lead Him to disown us and evict us. And what about people such as Mortaci, who believed in a Universal Power found in nature, and who did not worship Israel's God nor attend the temple religious events?

I saw that Jesus seemed dedicated to changing the image of the Father that many of us carried in our hearts; he wanted our God to be approachable, understanding, forgiving, and encouraging, like the imaginary ideal father we all wished that we had had.

One day, my musings were interrupted when Andrew dropped back out of the band of men to join me. "Shalom, David," he said, "and a good day to you as well." "Shalom," I replied, "and any day on the road with Jesus is a good one, despite the cold weather."

We walked for a while in silence. Andrew could best be described with one word, I thought: "rugged." He was tall and large-framed. His hair was bleached a reddish-blond from innumerable days in the sun while on the water fishing. His face was wind-burned and ruddy, and his huge hands were cracked and cut from the rigors of the fishing life. His fingernails were broken and jagged, and I noticed small scars all over his body.

Suddenly he broke the silence and blurted out: "What do you make of all of this?" I could tell that it had taken some courage on his part to ask the question. "Make of what?" I asked, stalling for time. "Of this call from Jesus," he said. "All of us have been torn away from everything we knew, and now we don't even know where we're going."

"Tell me about how it started for you," I said, still having no good answer to his question. "I was a follower of John the Baptist," Andrew began, "and when Jesus appeared at the Jordan River to be baptized, he exuded a presence that was very powerful and almost other-worldly. I wanted to know more about him, so my friend and I approached him. He invited us to join him for the day, and I was mesmerized by his words. Later, I found Simon, my brother, and told him that we had met the Messiah. However, when we went back looking for him the next day, he was nowhere to be found."

"Several weeks later, we were fishing," he said, "Simon, and me. Our father owns the business, and we work for him. We had fished all night and hadn't gotten a single fish. We both were in a foul mood, and neither one of us relished the fact that we had to report our failed attempts to our father. Jesus, whom it took a few minutes to recognize, came along with a large crowd pressing in around him. He asked Simon for the use of the boat, and Simon and I rowed him out a few feet from shore, where he began to teach the people about God and about the proper way to live one's life."

"When he was done teaching the crowds, this Jesus, who obviously wasn't a fisherman, instructed us to row out into deeper water and try again to catch fish. We both thought he was crazy, but Simon had the intuition that there might be more to it than a stranger's whimsy, so he agreed to do as directed." Andrew continued: "We pulled out a short distance and let down the nets, mostly to satisfy Jesus and not expecting to catch anything, since we determined that the fish had moved to a different part of the lake."

"When we went to haul in the net, it would not budge, and we thought it was caught on a stone on the bottom of the lake. But Simon and I kept heaving on it, and we could feel things moving in the net. We called out to James and John, and they helped us drag the net to shore. It was filled to the breaking point with fish. Simon is quicker to grasp things than I am; he fell to his knees, and inspired by who knows what, he said: 'Leave me, Lord. I am a sinful man.' Jesus then said 'Do not be afraid. From now on you will be catching men'."

"Simon then moored the boat and walked away from his lifetime's work. I stood there, baffled and stunned, but since I had been the first to leave John and follow Jesus, and since I usually accompanied Simon wherever he went, I too started down the path with Jesus. James and John came with us. Shortly thereafter, Philip and Nathaniel joined us."

"That's quite a story," I noted, "and now you are wondering what it is all about." "Yes," said Andrew, "I am off balance and a bit scared. Fishing was simple and predictable. Our father was of course very angry about our departure, but the huge number of fish we caught made a large sum of money for him, and he realized he could get hired help who would work for less than we received, meaning that he would make more profits. As I said, Jesus moved down the shoreline with us and invited James and John to join us. They too dropped everything and followed along. Their father, Zebedee, was furious and began to roar loudly. Jesus thereafter called James and John 'the sons of thunder'."

"I assured our father that we would be back soon," Andrew continued, "but now I'm not so sure. Jesus is moving along at a steady pace, teaching the growing crowds and now, healing people as well. This thing could get out of control sometime soon. I don't know if he's a magician or what, but none of us have ever seen anybody do what he does." Andrew paused: "Some say he is a prophet sent from God, perhaps the most powerful prophet to ever walk the earth. Since John's death, all of John's followers have suddenly switched over to Jesus. Each time we approach a village, it's like they've already heard of him and are eager to drop what they're doing and follow him, sometimes for days."

"You've been spared the pressure of the crowds these first few days, but you will see them soon enough. Their following, almost suffocating us, will resume as soon as we reach the more populated region of Galilee, and we're almost there already. This area is home for me," he continued, "and I'm wondering if I should leave the band and return to my fishing. Simon says that if I go, I'll have to go back alone; he's staying with Jesus."

"I see," I said. "And why do you think he called you in the first place?" "I think he really wanted Simon," Andrew answered, "and I was just included as kind of an afterthought. Simon is a natural leader, and while he can be impetuous and do rash things, he's also very intuitive, and courageous too. With polishing, he can be a valuable ally." "Jesus doesn't seem to do anything capriciously," I replied, "and for some reason perhaps only known to him, he wanted you in the group also. You must have abilities he values."

Andrew shrugged and walked along in silence. He finally said: "I don't think I have any unusual abilities, let alone abilities Jesus might value. I am uneducated and only fit for hard, manual labor. My needs are simple, and my knowledge about the ways of God is scant. We are not a religious family, but instead we are focused on money and survival."

"Ah," I said, "I think I might have an answer. You are just like the rest of the people who are clamoring to connect with Jesus. They too are struggling to make enough money to survive. They will identify with you immediately, because you're one of them. With your hard-working background and your rugged appearance, they will know that you have experienced what they're experiencing. When you speak to them, they will listen."

"That's just the point," Andrew replied, "I don't know how to speak, and if I did, I wouldn't know what to say." "Be yourself," I advised, using the same words Jesus had used to assuage my doubts, "just be yourself. Talk simply to them about the things Jesus is trying to teach them and you too. Love of God and neighbor are not difficult concepts to communicate. With your rugged appearance they will look up to you and hear you." Andrew shook his head. "You make it sound easy," he said, "but I am still unconvinced. Maybe I'll just slip away when everyone is sleeping; life will be much simpler then."

"You'll miss the greatest event in human history," I said. "What's that?" he asked. "The coming of the Messiah," I said, "our God made flesh who has come to redeem us." Andrew didn't answer, but instead looked at the ground, mulling over my words. I looked at the ground too, and observed that Andrew's sandals were in tatters. "Your sandals need fixing," I said. "I need new ones," he responded, "but I can't afford them and I don't want to ask Judas for the money." I reached in my bag and produced my new set. "Here," I said, "take these." "Oh, I couldn't do that," Andrew replied, "these old ones will be fine." "Then borrow these new ones and I will repair yours for you; then we can swap back and you'll have a like-new pair." Andrew reluctantly accepted. We stopped near a flat rock, and the exchange was made. The new sandals fit him well.

I already liked Andrew a lot; he was humble, honest and sincere. "I want you to stay," I said, "I need a friend and you can be that friend. I admire your simplicity. Stay. We'll talk together." "I'll think about it," he said quietly, and then left to rejoin the other men.

AFFIRMATION

That evening I sat in the shade of an old olive tree, working on Andrew's sandals. The problem was as I had expected: the sandal-maker had used decent leather but inferior thread, and the thread had rotted from Andrew's sweat and had broken in several places.

I first removed all of the old thread, using the little awl I had in my carry-bag. I saw that with some ingenuity, I could re-use all of the old leather pieces. Rising, I began looking under the olive tree, which was no longer pruned nor cultivated, and soon I had gleaned a large handful of wild, over-ripe olives. I had watched Judas the cook produce olive oil by mashing mature olives, and I followed suit, squeezing a small amount of oil into my cup.

I painstakingly worked the oil into all of the leather pieces, noting that the salt and grime rose to the surface and could be wiped away with a handful of grass which I gathered for the job. When I finished, the leather was soft, clean, and very pliable, almost like new.

I was just starting to sew the pieces back together when Jesus appeared and sat down beside me. He nodded affirmatively and said: "You're doing a good job." "Oh, it's nothing," I responded, "I've been working on leather most of my life." "No," he said, "I mean with your new calling." I sat in silence and then resumed sewing, not knowing where he was going with the conversation. "Because of you, Andrew is going to stay with us and not go back to his home. He will be a great witness and worker for our God."

"I really didn't do anything for him," I responded, "I hardly even knew what to say to him." "David, David, David," Jesus smilingly scolded, "you are so hard on yourself and you don't give yourself any credit. It's all part of that lack of self-esteem from which you've suffered. From now on, I want you to take humble credit for your abilities and for your contributions. Celebrate your gifts, and give praise and thanks to God, the Giver."

Jesus continued: "But you're right in one respect: it is not anything you said that changed Andrew's mind." "Oh, the sandals," I said, "I would have fixed the sandals for anyone. It's what I know how to do and I saw it as a chance to provide loving service to another."

"It's not the sandals, either," Jesus said, waiting for his words to sink in. I was now fully perplexed, so I again sat in silence, looking down at my work as I continued sewing. Jesus finally went on: "You listened to Andrew and accepted him and his doubts without judgment. In fact, you shared some of your same feelings. That was his turning point."

"Remember my advice," Jesus continued; "these men need someone to talk to, to share their feelings with, someone who cares about them and listens to them, someone who is present for them and is concerned about them. They need an accepting grandfather who will always be available for them and who will love them unconditionally. You're that person," Jesus went on, "and this is the mission I have given you. Also, your holiness is not wasted on these men; they see that you are prayerful and also sincere in your search for God, and they admire that. Continue being yourself, David, and all will be well."

CALEB

Jesus stayed with me and watched me sew. I used up the last of my thread on the final seam, and the sandals were fully restored. "I didn't bring enough thread," I said to no one in particular. "There you go again," Jesus said gently. "You are so hard on yourself. You brought exactly the right amount of thread, and you have put it to good purpose. David, you must work hard at eradicating the paralyzing self-criticism from your words. You are enough and your talents are enough and your actions are enough. Believe me."

"We are going to rest here tomorrow," Jesus added; "go into the nearby town and find a merchant named 'Caleb,' and he will have the thread that you need to fix more sandals. My Spirit will be with you, so that you will be able to handle whatever you encounter." With that Jesus rose, patted me on the arm, and said: "You are a good man, David, and a blessing to me. You just need to believe in yourself and in your power to promote God's kingdom in your own way. You are special, and only you can do what I've called you to do." As he left, he smiled and added: "Believe in yourself as much as I believe in you."

I sat for a long time, pondering his words. He was right: it was not my custom to think good thoughts about myself. Instead, I was always painfully aware of my faults and shortcomings, of the times I wished I had said or did something but instead missed the opportunity. His request that I think more highly of myself was reasonable and healing.

I resolved to work at reducing the limiting, self-deprecating thoughts that often filled my mind. I was grateful that Jesus saw the good in me, even when I sometimes didn't.

The next morning, I headed toward the nearby town, Shadow walking alongside of me. I had strong qualms about the mission, since I had no money with which to buy thread, but Jesus had given me specific guidance on how to proceed and I trusted him, so I journeyed in faith, not ever guessing the magnitude of the adventure upon which I was embarking.

When I entered the town, I ask a passerby where I might find Caleb's shop. The man gave me a strange look, but then gave me directions. As I approached the shop, a small, tired-looking, beaten-down man appeared in the doorway. From his appearance I sensed that he might be ill-tempered and mean-spirited, and my hunch was correct. "What do you want?" he snarled in a most unfriendly manner. "I need some thread," I responded as warmly as possible, "and the Master said that I would find it here." "I have no master but Caesar," he said sarcastically, "but I'll sell you thread. How much money do you have?"

"None," I replied, "but I will work to pay for it. Perhaps you have some sandals that need repairing." The man looked down at his bare, badly cracked feet. "I cannot afford food," he said bitterly, "let alone sandals." I looked at the thread he was trying to sell. It was discolored from long exposure to the sun and covered with road dust as well. The few other items of merchandise on his make-shift sales table were equally faded and unattractive. I stood there silently, not knowing what else to say. He finally spoke again.

"Who is this 'master' of yours?", he asked. "Jesus of Nazareth," I replied boldly. "Ah, the sorcerer," he said; "I have heard of him and his magical tricks inspired by the devil." I stood there stunned and initially afraid, but then I found my voice and responded: "He is a holy man who only does good, loving things using the power of God residing in him. The evil one flees from Jesus because he knows that Jesus is the Messiah sent from God."

"Can he heal my lame son?" the man asked cynically. "Why don't you come and meet him and ask him for yourself?" I said. "I will take you to him. Bring your son along too." The man reentered his small hut and emerged with a small boy who had a badly withered right leg. "Aren't you going to put your wares away where they'll be safe?", I asked. "No, nobody wants these things anyway," he said. Out of the corner of my eye, I saw him slyly slip a ball of thread into a hidden pocket, hoping I didn't see him do it.

We wended our way back up the hillside, the man carrying the small boy. Before long, I caught sight of Jesus, praying alone in a cool, green glade of trees. Jesus rose and greeted us; "Hello, Caleb, and shalom; you are welcome here. Shalom, David." Caleb was obviously taken aback by the fact that Jesus knew his name, and he was even more surprised when Jesus reached out and took Caleb's son into his arms in a loving embrace.

"What brings you here?" Jesus said warmly, while still holding the boy, "what can I do for you?" "I would like his leg healed," Caleb replied. "You worship Janus, the pagan Roman Gatekeeper God," Jesus said, "why don't you pray to him for this healing?"

Caleb looked at the ground. "I pretend to worship Janus because the Romans give me what scant business I have," he answered truthfully. "Janus has never done anything for me except to leave me in the misery and hardship my wife, son and I endure every day."

Jesus nodded, the child still comfortably ensconced in his arms. "She's not your wife," Jesus said matter-of-factly, looking knowingly into Caleb's eyes. Caleb looked at the ground again. "How do you know so much about me?" he asked. Jesus ignored the question and continued: "She's a slave you purchased only to satisfy your carnal desires."

"So you won't heal my son because I'm sinful," Caleb stated. Again, Jesus parried the question by asking: "Do you believe I can heal him?" Caleb thought for a while, desperately wanting to say "Yes" but not wanting to be caught lying again. Without knowing what prompted me, I stepped closer and said "Caleb wants to believe in you, but he doesn't know how to yet." "Well said, David," Jesus replied, "I know that to be true."

He turned to Caleb; "Perhaps it is you that needs the healing," Jesus said to him. "Yes, perhaps it is me," Caleb responded. "What must I do to be saved?" "Love your Father, the God of Israel, with your whole heart and soul, and love your neighbor as yourself." "My neighbor hates me," Caleb remarked. "That is because you lust after his wife and exchange lewd glances with her," Jesus responded, "and he knows what is in your heart." For yet another time, Caleb looked down at the ground, unable to meet Jesus' gaze. "You truly know my heart," Caleb said, "is there possibly any hope for me to be saved?"

"Caleb, how badly do you want salvation?" Jesus asked. "Very badly," Caleb said, "I am lost and miserable and my life is going nowhere. Also, we are truly starving to death. We have no food left, and no hope of getting any." "And do you believe that I have the way to eternal life?" Jesus queried. Caleb paused again, looking off into the distance. "Help him believe," I found myself saying, "down deep he is a good man and sincerely wants salvation. Be merciful, Jesus, and help him see the way to eternal life."

"Is this what you want, Caleb?" Jesus said. "Yes, and I want the lad to be healed." "Why do you want the child to be healed?" Jesus asked. Caleb fell to the ground, sobbing. "Not for good reasons, Lord" he said, "not for good reasons. I want him healed so that he's not a disgrace to the family, dragging his leg around like he does, and so that I don't have to care for him for the rest of my life. I'm just tired and hopeless," he added.

Jesus nodded. "I admire your truthfulness, Caleb," Jesus said, "and I will give you the formula for a satisfying life here in this world and for eternal life in the hereafter." From where he lay on the ground, Caleb clutched Jesus around the knees and said: "Oh, I want those things more than anything in the world. Please help me and tell me what to do."

"First, go home and court your mate," Jesus said. "Be kind and respectful to her, and treat her like an equal instead of like a slave. Do thoughtful things for her, and share the workload with her. It will take time, but you can earn her love, and when you do, become betrothed to her in the proper manner and take her as your lawful wife."

"Go to temple each Sabbath," Jesus continued, "not because it's a duty but because it's a privilege. Praise God, ask for His forgiveness as you forgive your enemies, and ask him for what you need. Pray to Him each morning and evening, and think about Him during the day. Live your life as if He is lovingly watching your every action, for indeed He is."

"Next, make peace with your neighbor. Let him know that you are sorry for former misunderstandings and transgressions. Do kind things for him, and show him that you regret your past actions. This too will take time, but it will occur if you are sincere."

"Next, merge your business with Ephraim's." "What?" Caleb interrupted, "he is my competitor and the reason I am not thriving." "You alone are the reason you are not thriving, Caleb" Jesus responded; "you have been lazy and have lacked motivation. The few coins you get from the Romans will not sustain you or your family. Ephraim is a tired old man, and he has no heir to whom to leave his business. Close your shop, go to work for him, labor honestly and diligently, and when Ephraim dies, the business will be yours, and a good business too." "You're right on all counts," Caleb said, "so right."

"And what about the boy?" Caleb asked, nodding toward the child in Jesus' arms. "You neglect the lad," Jesus replied. "The only attention he gets from you is when he displeases you by limping, so he has no motivation to try to not limp. Now his bones are shriveled and his muscles are atrophied." "Will you heal him?" Caleb asked hopefully. "No, but you will yourself if you believe in me and have faith in my instructions," Jesus said.

Caleb nodded. Jesus continued: "Each night at dusk, you must walk with the boy to the river and back. You must not rush the boy, because this will be a taxing activity for him, and there will be some pain involved as well. Lovingly wash his leg in the water while you are there. You must do this faithfully for a year, never missing a day, and by the end of the year, if you have been true to this undertaking, your son will be healed."

Caleb stood up. A new strength seemed to come over him. "Is that everything?" he asked. Jesus shook his head. "One more thing," Jesus said; "Take the lad to the temple and consecrate him to God as your firstborn. Later he will be the salvation of many."

Jesus smiled encouragingly. Caleb met Jesus' gaze. "I can do these things, and I will do them, I swear," he said, "but I need to know that God forgives me for my past sins and that I am starting over with a clean slate. How can I know that I am truly forgiven?"

"By the Name and Grace of my Father, I assure you that your sins are forgiven, and that if you do as I have asked, you and your family will be with me in paradise," Jesus said.

"Praise you and thank you, Jesus" Caleb said, "You are truly the Messiah, the son of God, bringing good news to all of us suffering wretches who need hope in our lives. I swear again, I will do as you say, and I will live." He hugged Jesus and then me, wished us both shalom and good health, and tenderly took the boy back into his own arms. As he walked by me, he slipped the thread into my hand. "I wish it were more," he said, "but this is all I have. Think of me and pray for me as you are mending the world's sandals."

THOMAS

As Caleb strode briskly away, a smile on his face and his son lovingly held in his arms, I couldn't resist my own curiosity, and turning to Jesus, I asked: "Will he make it, Jesus, will he be able to do all that you've asked him to do?" "He will struggle," Jesus replied, "and he will fail at times, but in the end he will make it, and the boy will walk freely, and someday help spread the news of the kingdom of God as you and I are doing. Yes, he will make it, thanks in large measure to you and your courage in speaking up to him."

I opened my mouth to protest, but remembering Jesus' admonition to me from earlier in the day, I closed it again without saying anything. "Good catch," he said good-naturedly, "there's hope for you yet!" He gave me a playful tap on my forehead and walked off.

I dozed off in the cool shade, but soon sensed someone in my presence. I opened my eyes to see Thomas towering over me. "Is he the Messiah?" he asked bluntly, failing to greet me or even ease into the conversation with small talk and pleasantries. At first I wanted to stall for time by answering his question with another question, but I quickly decided instead to adopt his style and answer in kind. "Yes," I said, "he is the Messiah."

"I thought you'd say that," Thomas countered, "but I'm afraid you're mistaken." "Oh," I said, "why do you say that?" "Because he doesn't fit the mold," Thomas responded; "he has no military capability, no religious stature, no political connections, no resources."

I was immediately ready to provide a sensible argument against Thomas' position, but something Jesus said about "listening" entered my mind, and I instead said nothing. After a brief silence, Thomas continued: "Jerusalem should be his power base, and yet he couldn't wait to leave there and head to Galilee, where there are as many pagans as there are true believers. He seems more at home here, and that doesn't make sense to me."

Thomas stared down at me quizzically; "don't tell me that you agree with those that say he is the Son of God," Thomas said. "Yes, I do" I said, and then fell silent again. Thomas sat down on the grass, looking very perplexed. "They say you are very learned when it comes to matters about God," he said, "so I'm surprised that you've been fooled by an itinerant teacher who has nothing and who has to beg for his lodgings and meals." Nearly biting my tongue in half, I continued to stay silent and looked at Thomas calmly.

We sat in silence, neither wishing to speak. After an interminable amount of time, Thomas broke the silence. "How do you know?" he asked. I sensed that he had stopped wanting to listen only to refute, and now was listening to understand, so I abandoned my tendency to want to stall again by asking "Know what?". I sensed that this was no time for playing games with a sincere seeker of the truth. "The Scriptures are full of prophecies about the Messiah," I said, "and Jesus fulfills them all perfectly, even to all of the circumstances surrounding his birth." "How do you know that," Thomas asked. "I was there, at his birth," I responded, "and everything happened exactly as it had been foretold. Shepherds and foreign royalty alike came to his birthplace, and angels sang in the sky."

Thomas looked at me hesitantly. "Can I believe you?" he asked quietly. "Yes," I said, "would you like to hear more?" He nodded. "What's wrong with most people's belief about the Messiah," I said, "is their expectation that the coming of the Messiah will herald the overthrow of the Romans and the resurgence of the Hebrew nation. Isaiah refutes that notion, suggesting that the Messiah will be a humble servant who will ultimately suffer greatly so that the people might be saved from eternal damnation."

"Yes, but he's supposed to be holy and righteous, and instead he associates with the lowliest of people," Thomas said. "Like us," I retorted. "No, no, no" Thomas exclaimed, "I mean with really sinful people." "Like us," I said again. Thomas stopped gesturing vehemently and his arm stayed poised in mid-air. I pressed my advantage: "We're all sinners, unworthy of the kingdom of God. Prostitutes, cheats, and even hypocritical religious leaders commit sins that are more obvious and therefore easier to condemn, but we are all just as sinful. By looking down on 'the real sinners' we can excuse our own sinfulness and feel better about ourselves by pretending we are better than they are."

"This conversation isn't going like I thought it would go," Thomas said. "I expected you to have logic behind your fidelity to him, but I thought I could win you over by argument. Now I see that your faith in him is well-grounded and very strong." "I was at his birth and his consecration," I said. "I met his parents. I studied under a devout priest who explained the prophecies about him for me. Undoubtedly he is the Messiah and the Son of God." "I'm not convinced," Thomas said, and with that he stood up and walked away.

WILDERNESS

The next day we left the main road that led to Nazareth and instead journeyed up a rough path into truly desolate country. I noticed that after only a few days, I was beginning to get accustomed to the rigors of climbing the mountains without becoming exhausted. Like the others, I had become a gleaner, always on the look-out for over-ripe fruit and vegetables that the harvesters had left behind. Judas, son of James and our cook, always seemed to manage to work wonders with such produce, so we all strove to provide it.

At noon, we stopped in the shade of a great cliff, looking down at the olive groves in the valley below. Lunch consisted of a small crust of bread, some dried fish, and a large amount of fresh water from a spring that issued from a crack in the mountain's wall.

Philip joined me, which pleased me because I had questions to ask him. "I don't know this area at all," I said, "but it seems like we are skirting around Nazareth. That surprises me, because it is Jesus' home town and he must have a lot of family and friends there." "Nazareth is not a safe place for Jesus," Philip replied; "he had a bad experience there a short time ago, and it's better that we all stay away from there and let things calm down."

"Would you please tell me everything you know about Jesus and his ministry from the very beginning?" I asked; "I don't know anything about what has transpired before my meeting with him on the Mount of Olives above Bethany just a short time ago."

"I'll tell you what I know," Philip responded. "Jesus started out by himself as an itinerant preacher, moving from town to town. I'm told that everyone that heard him was very impressed with his wisdom and with his passion for repentance. The people didn't know what to make of his assertion that the 'kingdom of God was at hand,' but they knew that Jesus was extraordinary, especially because of the aura of authority he exuded."

"He preached in many synagogues and was favorably received. Eventually he arrived at Nazareth, and was asked to preach on the Sabbath. Bear in mind that almost everyone present already knew him only as a carpenter, Joseph's son. Hearsay has it that his listeners therefore were pleasantly surprised by the soundness and wisdom of his words."

"He was then handed the scroll containing the prophecies of Isaiah, and finding Isaiah's predictions regarding the Messiah, he read them, closed the scroll, and announced that that day, in their presence, the prophecies were being fulfilled. The people were stunned, and before they could react, Jesus told them that he did not expect them to believe him because no prophet is accepted in his own land. I have a certain amount of sympathy for the people," Philip continued; "imagine seeing someone sawing boards for twenty-plus years who is now proclaiming himself as the Messiah. It was pretty hard to accept. At any rate, a couple of bullies in the congregation started yelling and inciting the others, and the attendees who had been impressed with Jesus a few moments before now became an unruly and dangerous mob. They dragged Jesus out of the synagogue and out to a high cliff, where they intended to kill him, but no one had the courage to actually do it."

"Jesus walked through their midst and left the town, and I'll be surprised if he ever returns there. He headed for Capernaum, my home town, which became his base of operations, and from there he preached along the shores of Lake Galilee, also known as the Sea of Galilee or Lake Gennesaret. The Romans call it Lake Tiberias. It was at this time that Jesus called Simon and Andrew, James and John, and myself and Nathaniel."

"Immediately after our calling, we all started out together for a wedding feast at Cana. Mary, the mother of Jesus was there, as were many of our family and friends. It was a gala affair, with much joy and celebration, and it lasted several days. Many people drank heavily, and the married couple were about to be embarrassed by running out of wine. I did not see it with my own eyes, but hearsay has it that Mary asked Jesus to remedy the problem, and while he momentarily seemed hesitant to do so, he met with the wine steward and there was suddenly several forty-gallon jars filled with the finest wine."

"From Cana, our little band headed back to Jerusalem for the Passover. Jesus became noticeably preoccupied, almost on the edge of anxiety, if that is possible. Word of the clash in Nazareth had reached Jerusalem, and some members of the Sanhedrin were already discussing Jesus and his teaching and his works among themselves. Itinerant preachers were common and were tolerated, but when any of them attracted a sizable following, they were deemed a threat to the status quo and therefore watched closely.

As we traveled the long road back to Jerusalem, Jesus continued to preach and to heal people of all kinds of maladies. In truth, word of his works preceded him into Jerusalem."

"In Jerusalem, we proceeded to the temple, and the rottenness of the religious system which had transformed the temple into an economic enterprises seemed to disturb him greatly, and he spoke out freely and vehemently against the religious leaders. Jesus continued to preach and to heal people in Jerusalem for a few days, and in the meantime some members of the Sanhedrin had a sincere desire to know more about him, to the point that one of them, Nicodemus, sought him out after dark to talk to him in secret."

"We then spent some time in Judea, where Jesus preached repentance and instructed us to baptize all who wished to be saved, just as his cousin John was doing elsewhere. After a while, supporters of Jesus informed us that the Sanhedrin was watching his movements and that there were spies in the crowd, noting his every word, so we then slipped away to the home of Lazarus, Martha and Mary, Jesus' friends in Bethany, where we rested for several days. That is when you met Jesus on the Mount Olives and chose to follow him."

"We don't really know where Jesus is going next nor what he is trying to accomplish. It's just that he has such a magnetic personality and convincing message that we all choose to follow him and serve him in whatever way he wants us to."

I sat in silence for a while, wondering of what use I could be to Jesus, despite the briefing Jesus had already given me about my part in his ministry. Philip seemed to read my thoughts. "You will be a stabilizing influence," he said. "We are all inexperienced, young, and even a bit irreverent, and you will help us grow, mature, and become holy."

JUDAS ISCARIOT

I thanked Philip for the lengthy briefing on the events that had transpired before I met Jesus on the mountain. The day was unseasonably warm, and as Philip rose to leave, he informed me that the group would be staying in this cool, shaded spot until the following morning. I got to my feet and gave Philip a warm embrace; I was fond of him, and he knew it. He tended to want to look for the deeper meaning of events, and I admired that.

As I sat in the shade at the spring, a shadow blocked the sun, and I looked up to see Judas Iscariot standing over me, a cloth sack in his hands. I could tell he was uncomfortable. "This is for you," he said, and placed the sack on my lap. I opened it and was overjoyed to find the cup and plate that I had given him days before, and that he had promptly sold.

When I recovered my senses, I said "But this was a gift for you from me, Judas." "Yes," he replied, "but I didn't respect it or appreciate it. Just like me to always be thinking about how to get more money. The look on your face when I told you I sold these items made me realize how much I had hurt you. When we passed back through the town where I had sold them, I found the merchant and bought them back. I'm truly sorry."

I stood, tears streaming down my cheeks, and embraced him. "The loss of these items was very painful," I said, "but I have forgiven you." "Yes, I expected that you had," he said, "because that's the way you are. I will try to do better in the future." With that, he broke the embrace and looked at me again. "I am truly sorry," he said, and walked away.

TIBERIAS

I sat back down in the shade near the cool spring, contentedly mending another pair of sandals. I had discovered yet another pleasant surprise: no matter how much of Caleb's thread or how many of the leather scraps I used, there was always enough in the bottom of my carry-bag to fix the next pair of sandals. My meager resources were inexhaustible.

Evening came, and Andrew brought the serving pan of dinner to me and ladled out a generous portion of fish stew onto my plate, along with a little baked fruit tart for dessert. "Our cook is a magician," he said, "seemingly making wonderful meals from nothing. The food is always good, and there's plenty for everyone. I don't know how he does it."

"I'm glad you're here," Andrew said, patting me on the shoulder, and he then turned away to take the serving pan to the remainder of the men. I realized that I had been served first, which always humbled me. "The privileges of old age," I thought to myself.

Evening fell, and I didn't move from my spot. When it became too dark to work on the sandals any longer, I leaned back onto the side of the mountain and watched a wonderful sunset. I had plenty to think about. Philip's recounting of Jesus' saga before I joined him had been an awakening, in that I was suddenly aware that Jesus stirred up resentment and controversy by boldly confronting people with the truth of his message, a truth that many did not want to hear. And, as a potential threat to the Sanhedrin, he was surely in danger.

I also pondered the latest joyous encounter with Judas. I examined my conscience and prayed that the last vestiges of resentment that I had about him would be removed, since he was obviously contrite. While I might not like his behavior, I prayed fervently that I could be able to love him as a fellow sojourner, despite his faults and imperfections.

The sunset segued into dusk and the dusk into darkness, with millions of stars visible in the sky. I reclined on my back with my carry-bag as my pillow, and I thought about all that had already transpired in the relatively short time in which I had followed Jesus. With my cloak as a blanket, I sent my night prayers into the heavens and fell asleep.

I awoke in the middle of the night with the sense that I was being watched. I rose up on one elbow and saw Shadow standing there, apparently wanting me to follow him. Since I had pledged to always heed his signals, I stuffed my meager possessions into my carry-bag and started up the path behind him. Because there was ample starlight and moonlight I was able to easily traverse the rocky terrain by always walking where he walked.

When we reached the top of the ridge line, I could see a figure illuminated in the faint light. It was Jesus, of course, and I had been summoned to meet with him. He had a small fire going, and it had already burned down to coals. "Shalom," he said, "please let me borrow your cups and plates." I didn't miss the significance of his words about "cups and plates." "Shalom," I said, embracing him, "You don't miss a thing, do you?" He smiled in response and served us both a small breakfast in the pre-dawn darkness.

"That was a beautiful encounter you had with Judas," he said. "Judas has a battle being waged within him, and he is torn between good and evil. I appreciate anything you can do to help, such as today when you let him know you love him and have forgiven him."

Then, as usual, he caught me totally off-guard with a question. "Have you thought about returning home?" he asked. I reflected on his question, and then answered: "not even for a moment." We sat in silence, and then I continued. "The only thing to do there is mend sandals and be lonely and eventually die alone. Here I am content and somewhat useful and very fulfilled, and I am tremendously privileged to be serving the Son of God."

"Do you have any doubts about who I am?" he continued. "When I first heard abut you, you were still in your mother's womb," I replied, "and I had doubts then until Zechariah spent countless hours explaining the prophecies to me. When your birth fulfilled all of them, all doubts vanished. I firmly believe with all of my heart and soul that you are the Messiah, the Son of God, and I am privileged to serve you in whatever manner I can."

What happened next surprised me greatly. Jesus began to weep, and through his tears he said: "Your faith in me strengthens me more than you know. I look back and see you dutifully trudging along, and I draw strength from your commitment to me and my work. You are essential to the success of my ministry, and it is important that you are still fully committed." "I am with you as long as I am physically able," I said, "but I worry about my stamina." "I will give you sufficient strength for the journey," Jesus replied.

We sat in silence. I had been so focused on Jesus and on the small fire that was warming us that I hadn't as yet looked around. Jesus had obviously chosen this spot carefully. We were on the crest of a high ridge, facing east. Way below us, a few lights shown from the city of Tiberias, and beyond them, the bobbing lanterns on the fishing boats indicated that men were already at work on Lake Galilee, trying to eke out a meager living.

As the first pink rays of sunrise appeared, Jesus broke the silence: "It's too bad that so many are asleep and are missing all of this." "Yes," I replied, "most of the people haven't risen yet." As soon as I had spoken, I realized that I had made a mistake by replying too soon, and that I had missed the deeper point that Jesus was making. "I'm sorry," I said, "I see now that you were speaking about people being existentially asleep at all times, both day and night." "Yes," Jesus replied, "I am mourning the fact that our loving Father gives us all of this beauty to hearten us, but most people get caught up in daily survival and miss the fact that they have a loving Father who cares for them. That is my mission," he continued, "to bring people to know and love our beneficent Father."

"Let's pray," he said, and with that he extended his hand and helped me too my feet. Still holding each other's hand, we extended our arms to the heavens and chanted our morning prayers as we watched the pink hues change to a myriad of different morning colors, ending with the appearance of the tip of the sun on the horizon. Below us, Tiberias began to come alive. With his goal of honoring Caesar, Herod Antipas had chosen this location well; Tiberias was a jewel in the morning sun, with Lake Galilee gleaming beyond it.

The scene was breathtaking, and Jesus and I stood drinking it in for a long time. Further north we could see the beautiful town of Magdala and beyond it a glimpse of Capernaum. I wanted the moment to never end; here I was, holding the hand of the Son of God and praying with him to his father and my Father, the most moving event in my life.

Eventually we sat back down. By now it was fully daylight. Jesus looked at me intently and began to speak. "Starting today," he said, "my real work begins. The crowds will come and press in upon us, and we will no longer have times like this to share together. Our band of followers grows larger each day, and today I will summon the twelve men I want to accompany me at all times. I want you to be present at the summoning, and of course, I want you to continue being with us from now on, doing what you're doing now, which is to set a holy tone and a sacred atmosphere for this entire undertaking."

"The men will need a steadying influence more than ever, and doubts will surely assail them as events unfold in a manner they hadn't expected. I'm entrusting you with the spiritual care of these men, especially when I cannot be fully present for them. Love them as I love them, and continually reassure them that they are indeed on the right path."

With that, Jesus rose and helped me to my feet. Embracing me, he again told me how much my presence meant to him personally, and also to the men, although they might not always express their appreciation. "Shalom, Elder David," he said; "I have infinite trust in you and I value you greatly." "Shalom, Jesus," I said, and he turned and walked away.

TWELVE PLUS ONE

I sat pondering all that Jesus had said and savoring the exquisite view below me to the east. Our original small band had grown each day, and now there was a large number of people walking with us. Some came for a few hours, others for a few days, and others more or less permanently. Jesus' prediction of even more followers was about to come true. Perhaps the biggest change to our arrangement was the appearance of several women who joined our band and seemed committed to serving Jesus however they might. I reflected on how fast things were moving and I questioned how it would all turn out.

I must have dozed for a while, because the next thing I knew, Jesus reappeared with a large number of his followers, both men and women. He bade them all to sit down on the mountainside, and he chose a rock seat to my left and a few feet in front of me. That choice of a seating spot was obviously premeditated, and it put me in a position of honor at Jesus' right side and slightly behind him. I was again humbled by his respect for me.

When everyone was seated and had become quiet, Jesus began addressing the assembly. He repeated some of what he had shared with me earlier: that his work would now start in earnest, that there would be large crowds and a certain degree of chaos, and that there would be good times and bad times in the future, including the salvation of many people but also the need for him to suffer at the hands of the established leaders in Jerusalem. I saw that his listeners were surprised and somewhat scared by his words about suffering.

He said that he welcomed everyone's faithfulness and support, and that he hoped it would continue. He then added that his ministry had come to a point where he needed a reliable group of men who would become constant companions and co-workers for the duration of his ministry, however long that might be. He pointed out that that would mean a near-total change from their lives as they had known it, including a permanent break from their former jobs, and protracted absences from their families and friends, perhaps indefinitely.

Jesus then said that he would call each person's name, and that that person would have as long as he or she needed to decide whether or not they could make the commitment Jesus was seeking. If they decided to accept the designation of "apostle," they were to come forward and pledge their loyalty to Jesus and their commitment to his ministry.

After a moment, he began by calling forward Simon, whom he renamed "Peter;" Peter sprang to his feet and rushed forward, promising his eternal fidelity to Jesus and his work. Next came Andrew, then James and John, then Philip and Bartholomew (called Nathaniel), and finally Matthew and Thomas, James (son of Alphaeus) and Simon (the patriot), Judas (son of James) and Judas Iscariot. I noted that Jesus had called them forward in the order that he had first chosen them at the outset of his ministry, but I wondered then if there was more to the selection process, and especially to the calling forward of Peter first.

Jesus told the rest of the members of the crowd how much he appreciated their support and loyalty, and he welcomed them to stay with him as his disciples. The crowd then started back down the mountain, with the apostles following and Jesus and I in the rear.

SMITTEN AND SMOTE

I started my descent, walking a short distance behind Jesus as was my wont. I knew he appreciated the brief moments of solitude that he experienced at such times, and I enjoyed my time alone as well. I know that we were both highly introspective, and such times gave each of us the opportunity to pray and to reflect on all that was happening.

From the expressions on their faces, I knew that members of the crowd had various reactions to what they had just witnessed. Some were obviously disappointed that they had not been chosen as apostles, while others were visibly relieved that they had not been challenged to make such a huge and open-ended commitment to serve as an apostle. Even the newly-chosen apostles had mixed looks on their faces; some were exuberant as they strolled along, while others were more pensive, somber, and even a bit frightened.

As we descended on the rocky path in this arid, desolated spot, I saw Jesus looking to his left above him, and following his gaze, I saw a small child sitting on a ledge perilously close to a steep drop-off. Without hesitation and unseen by those in front of him, Jesus began to climb up to the child, and I clamored up the mountainside behind him.

What happened next was unexpected; I wouldn't have been surprised if Jesus had stood and talked to the child, or even bent over to be closer to it, but instead he got down on the ground in the dirt with the child and began investigating what it was the child was doing.

I sat down nearby on a rock to catch my breath and watch. The child was a girl of about four years old, badly emaciated from malnutrition and covered with pus-filled, infected sores. She was barefoot and her tattered clothes were little more than rags. She was very dirty and her hair was matted and snarled. She was the epitome of total parental neglect.

Behind her there was a small, shallow cave in the mountainside, and a hollow-eyed man and his wife sat inside on rocks in the shade. They were like the child: dressed in rags, filthy, emaciated, and sickly. I wondered how they had managed to survive thus far.

I watched as Jesus and the child were fascinated with something on the ground. I finally saw that they were watching a bug crawl along the ground, and both seemed entranced with the discovery. They crawled along behind the bug, talking as they proceeded. After a time, the little girl tired of the pursuit, and spying a weed in the rocks with a small blossom on it, she picked the flower and brought it to Jesus for his inspection. The two admired it for a while, and then the girl fearlessly crawled up on Jesus' lap, gave him the flower, leaned back in the crook of his arm, and contentedly fell asleep. I too closed my eyes for a brief nap, seizing the opportunity for some rest from the otherwise busy pace.

I opened my eyes after a short while and couldn't believe what I was seeing. Either I was imagining things, or the little girl, while she slept, had actually filled out a bit physically and seemed to have less infected sores. I rubbed my eyes and watched closely, but if there was any change going on with the child, it was slow and therefore imperceptible.

I closed my eyes, waited as long as I possibly could, and the reopened them again. I realized that I wasn't imagining things; the little girl was regaining her health while sleeping in Jesus' arms. With all that was waiting for Jesus in the valley below, I was surprised that he was tarrying so long while the little girl slept in his arms; if he wanted to heal her, he could have done so in an instant, but both he and she seemed perfectly at peace and in no hurry to do anything else. I repeated the process of closing my eyes, waiting, and then looking again, and eventually I knew she had regained total health.

At that point, something momentous happened to me, something snapped inside, and a wellspring of love flooded my body and overwhelmed me. Up until now, I had admired Jesus, respected him, appreciated him, was fond of him, and also feared him, but now something immense took over inside of me and I knew that I would never be the same.

I was deeply moved by the miracle I had witnessed; I had seen Jesus perform many miracles, but none with the patience and tenderness and compassion I had just seen. It was like Jesus could not walk by this child without reaching out to her with his healing touch, even though he had many other things to do that his followers would have deemed more important. My heart stretched to capacity with what I was feeling, and then it opened wide as an immeasurable inflow of love for this God-Man filled my whole being. Tears of joy streamed down my cheeks, and I knew that I had been profoundly changed. All of my concerns for myself, my physical health, my safety, and my future disappeared; there was only one thing left, and it was a transforming love for this wonderful Messiah.

"The child's name is Naomi," the woman said from inside the cave. "You are no doubt a holy man sent to us from God to restore our child to life." "Come, follow me," Jesus said, "and I will give you eternal life as well." "Tell us more about..." the woman started to say, until the man stopped her by delivering a heavy blow to her face which knocked her backward off of the rock on which she had been sitting. "Mind your place, woman" he said, and then, turning to Jesus, he spat on the ground and then continued: "You'd better leave now—you've already caused enough trouble."

Jesus rose, still holding the child in his arms. Using the last bit of energy she could summon, the woman dashed by the man before he could stop her and ran to Jesus' side. She clung to him, so weak from starvation that she could scarcely stand. "I will come with you, the child and I," she said, "there is nothing to hold us here except death."

The man stepped forward out of the cave menacingly, and glared at Jesus. Jesus calmly met the man's threatening look with a steady gaze. The man stopped advancing, and the stare-down ended when he lowered his eyes and spit on the ground. "Take them with you," he snarled, "they are worthless and this will mean two less mouths to feed."

Jesus turned and started back down the mountain, carrying the child in one arm and supporting the near-death woman with the other. I stood up and addressed the man: "He will do what he says and give you a new life too." I took a step toward him and said: "leave this desolate place and come with us, and he will heal your body and your soul."

The man spit on the ground again in disgust, and then reached over to pick up a lemon-sized stone from the ground. I suddenly realized that I had tarried too long, and that I was in serious physical danger at the hands of this near-starved and half-crazed man.

I turned and began to hasten down the path when the stone he threw hit me between the shoulder blades, knocking the wind out of me and driving me forward and onto my knees. I rolled over on the ground, and as I lay there gasping in an attempt to regain my breath, the man picked up a much larger stone and began advancing toward me. I was breathless and full of terror, knowing he intended to kill me. But I was paralyzed and unable to escape, so I lay there helplessly on the ground, expecting the worse.

The man was now only a short distance from me, and as he raised the stone over his head and prepared to kill me, Shadow manifested himself to the man and stood between him and me. The man was taken aback for a moment, and then amended his plans and aimed the stone at Shadow's head. He hurled the stone down with all of his weakened might, but since Shadow was pure spirit, the stone passed through the image of Shadow's head and harmlessly crashed onto the ground. The man rubbed his eyes in astonishment; he started searching for another stone, but then thought better of it and began retreating back into his cave, Shadow following him and driving him away from me. The man's amazement turned into terror, and he cried out pitifully: "Don't let your animal harm me; take it with you and depart." I was now able to get to my feet. "I forgive you," I replied, "and I will pray for you. I hope you reconsider and come join us. You'll always be welcome."

THE LESSON

I hobbled down the path, my upper back on fire with pain and my emotions running rampant. I would otherwise have found it very hard to forgive the man who had injured me so severely, but I was so full of love that any response other than forgiveness seemed inappropriate. So I prayed for the man as I trudged along, and also for his wife and child.

Despite Jesus' explicit prediction, I was not prepared for what appeared beneath me as I crested the final ridge above the valley below. A huge crowd had gathered and the scene had the semblance of a large, outdoor festival, which in fact it was. Some people had set up small tents, while others were cooking on small campfires of dried grass and twigs. Jesus and the apostles were mingling with the crowd, stopping here and there to converse.

I was not ready to join the maelstrom below, so I sat down in the shade of a large rock outcropping, Shadow lying vigilantly nearby. While Shadow had been an ever-visible, constant companion since he was given to me by Jesus, I now had a new appreciation of Jesus' suggestion that he would be far more than just company for me, but would in fact be a guardian charged with my safety. I wondered why Shadow hadn't sprung into action before the man had thrown the stone that hit me in the back, but I was grateful that he had saved my life just a few moments later by becoming manifest to the would-be killer. I felt deep sorrow that the angry, forlorn man had refused our invitation, and I resolved to reach out to him again if I were given the opportunity. Meanwhile, I prayed for him.

As evening approached I was still resting in the shade, my upper back still throbbing incessantly. A woman struggled up the hill, bringing me a warm bowl of a stew-like dish and a drink of cold water. Somehow, someone always made sure that, no matter where I was, I was located and served my evening meal first. I was appreciative for this ongoing gesture to my advanced age, and perhaps to my designation as "Elder," but I was also a bit chagrined that I was receiving such preferential treatment, being served even before Jesus and the apostles. Nevertheless, I thanked her warmly and she headed back down the hill.

Having women in the entourage created a new dynamic to the experience. Such basic needs as bathing and relieving oneself became more challenging, but on the other hand, some of the rough edges of the men seem to be replaced with courteous demeanors. There was no doubt that the women were equally faithful to Jesus and his ministry, and they provided for many of our temporal needs such as properly bandaging our wounds and administering healing herbs for the variety of illnesses which arose among us.

I rested on my side, being unable to lie on my aching back, and despite the pain, I continued to bask in the overflow of love that had filled every fiber of my body as I had watched Jesus love the young girl back to full health. Never in my life had I experienced such a powerful infusion of unconditional love, and I prayed that it would never lessen in its intensity. I knew that, more than ever, I was fully committed to Jesus and his ministry no matter where it led, and I was even stronger in my belief that he was the promised

Messiah. Still on my side, I laid my head on the ground and fell into an uneasy sleep.

Sometime after dark I was awakened by Shadow's stirring, and a cold fear immediately coursed through my body as I feared it was the man on the mountain returning to kill me. Shadow remained calm, however, and I was relieved when Jesus appeared and sat down next to me. As I sat up, he immediately put his hand on my back, and I felt intense heat emanating from the palm of his hand and concentrated on the painful wound on my back. In no time at all, the pain had disappeared completely, replaced by a warm, healing glow.

As usual, Jesus surprised me with his opening remark. "What you saw on the mountain with Naomi and her parents was a microcosm of my entire ministry," he said. "Our father in heaven loves each one of us and wants to hold each one of us tenderly and heal us with his infinite compassion and mercy, just as I healed Naomi. What you saw is what the Father offers all of us: unconditional love and complete healing of our souls. When people encounter this God, they are filled with love for him, just as you are. We must promote this image of the Father to the world," he continued; "that is our mission."

"The Father is not the harsh, judgmental despot that the religious leaders picture; He has been improperly portrayed, so people fear Him. We must undo such misgivings and encourage everyone to seek out the Father's healing, forgiveness, and total acceptance."

"How are the woman and child doing?" I asked. "The other women are ministering to them," Jesus responded, "Naomi is fine, and her mother will regain her health and will become a dedicated disciple and will give strong testimony to the Father's healing love."

"I want to go back and talk to the man," I said. "Perhaps now that he has had time to think about things, he will change his mind and come join us and rejoin his family."

Jesus shook his head back and forth vehemently. "I admire your zeal and also your willingness to forgive him and reach out to him again in love, but re-approaching him will be to no avail and in fact will place you in danger again. He has chosen death, both spiritually and physically, and he will most surely experience both in the near future."

"That too is a microcosm of my ministry," Jesus continued. "Many will be called; some will respond in faith and follow me, while others will turn a deaf ear and walk away. Some will grow angry and hateful, and will even try to physically harm us, sometimes succeeding. This is a ministry of loving service rather than of glorious triumph, and we will surely experience hardships and setbacks as we attempt to bring all to the Father."

"I will give all of the loving service I can," I said, "even if it means further physical suffering. I fell in love today," I continued, "a love different than but also stronger than any love I've ever felt. And what I fell in love with was Love itself, as I saw it flow through you to the child, and even to the mother and father. It was a powerfully moving experience that I will never forget. May I never lose the intensity of the love I feel now."

I laid back and began staring up at the stars. To my surprise, Jesus also reclined and reached out and took my hand, and so we both fell asleep. When I awoke, he was gone.

PONDERINGS

A young lad sprinted up the hill toward me in the early morning light, delivering a small loaf of bread filled with a delicious concoction of ground-up vegetables covered in sweet date honey. A spring emanated from the rocks under which I sat, and I had a refreshing drink of water to wash down my wonderful breakfast. I thanked the boy and blessed him and he ran back down the hill, carrying the dish and cup from the previous night's supper.

I had a lot to think about. I had seen Jesus perform so many miracles that there was a danger that I (and the others) would start taking such activities as commonplace. After yesterday's events, I realized that every miracle was intended to show us how the Father wanted us each to be whole and spiritually attracted to eternal life with Him. If this idea could successfully be conveyed to the multitudes, then everyone could be as full as I was of love for Love itself, as a result of witnessing the complete, loving healing of Naomi.

I was particularly curious as to why Jesus had taken my hand as I went to sleep, slept next to me for a while, and then disappeared into the night. I somehow knew that the gesture was meant to reassure and strengthen me, and perhaps reaffirm my presence in the group. Then an insight hit me and I immediately knew it was accurate: Jesus had not only meant to further prepare me for what was to come, but he was also drawing strength and support from the love and commitment I was feeling for him. I realized that his work was a huge drain on his energy, and that he also needed my love and support and prayer.

I was facing the glorious sunrise just appearing over Lake Galilee, and the love still bursting from my heart lent a new, powerful dimension to my morning prayers as I welcomed the sun and the day. It seemed that I had more than usual to pray about, including Naomi and her parents, forgiveness, intensified commitment to Jesus, etc.

I then sat in silence, hoping that the Spirit of God would enlighten me with additional insights about what I must do to more fully serve him. The previous day, lying on the hill with my upper back throbbing unmercifully, I had watched as the apostles had gathered and silenced the crowd, and then as Jesus had spoken to the assembled multitude at some length. I had longed to know what he had to say, but I was too far away to hear any of it.

Then the realization hit me: the nature of my participation in his ministry must change dramatically. No longer could I be detached from the contingent of apostles and disciples. No longer could I walk behind the group, alone with my thoughts and prayers. A lifetime of being private and reclusive must now end, and instead I must join the crowd and witness about Jesus and the Father in every way that I could. This is why Jesus had taken my hand as I drifted off to sleep: to strengthen me to become a changed man and to begin acting in a new way that would be difficult for me and even frightening to consider.

My life as a contemplative recluse was over, at least for the foreseeable future, and I was now being prompted to wade into the maelstrom of humanity and minister in a new way. These were uncharted waters, and I was fearful, but the call to change was unmistakable.

CHAOS

My morning prayer now took on a new dimension, and I pleaded with God to send His Spirit to direct me as I began doing something that was previously foreign to me and very uncomfortable for me to do. My prayer seemed richer because I now knew that I was totally dependent on God's grace and support to proceed forward. With renewed resolve and an even stronger trust in Jesus, I arose and headed down the hill into the unknown.

Despite all of the preparation Jesus had given us, I was nevertheless taken aback by what I encountered when I entered the crowd. There were needy persons with every physical, emotional, and spiritual problem imaginable. People clamored to get near Jesus. Pushing and shoving led to fights breaking out, with everyone wanting to get their needs met with little regard for anyone else in the multitude. Some instances of theft occurred, mostly involving one family stealing needed food and clothing from another. Chaos reigned!

People assailed me immediately, wanting money, or food, or an introduction to Jesus, or a miraculous healing if I could perform one, or any number of other things, all beyond my power to deliver. At first I turned away from such people, but eventually I realized that I had something to give them after all, so I began sitting with them and listening to their needs and to their life stories. Whenever possible, I blessed them and gave them encouragement, and they seemed calmer and more able to cope with their problems after they realized that I truly cared. I had found something I could do well: listen and love!

TRAGEDY

A few mornings later, I was enjoying my quiet prayer time as the newly-risen sun began to warm the day, when I observed the woman from the mountain approaching me with Naomi skipping along at her side. The child appeared full of health, vitality and joy, and her mother was getting well also, with the infected sores nearly healed, her hollowed cheeks beginning to fill out, and the dark circles under her eyes beginning to disappear. However, she was wearing a black shawl over her head, and that fact disturbed me.

As mother and daughter approached, Naomi broke away from her mother's grasp and ran to me, jumping into my lap with all of the youthful vigor she could muster. I was initially taken aback, but then I began savoring the experience, and I hugged her long and warmly.

"I'm Hara," the woman said; "I hope the child isn't bothering you." I thought back and realized that this was only the third child I had ever held in my sixty-plus years. The first was my own son, who had died in my arms, and the second was Jesus, both at his birth and at his consecration at the presentation in the temple. Naomi's exuberance and spontaneity felt wonderful, and I smiled at her as she made herself at home on my knee. "She's not bothering me at all," I said; "a child's spontaneous affection is something I've lacked for most of my life, and I now desire as much of such child-like love as I can get." The woman nodded, and spoke again: "I've come to thank you," she said, "you have given Naomi and me our lives back, and we will be eternally grateful for that."

"Not so," I replied. "It was Jesus who did all of that. I'm just a humble companion of his, although I must say that I am now forever changed by witnessing the healing process Naomi experienced in his arms as you and I watched. He is incredibly compassionate."

"I will believe in him and follow him whenever and wherever I can," she replied; "he truly does have the words of eternal life and the power to give it to us if we let him." "Your newfound faith is remarkable," I said, "and surely a gift from a loving God. I admire your willingness to leave everything to grasp the new life that he promises."

"Which leads me to the other reason for seeking you out," Hara said. "Have you heard the tragic news?" "No," I responded, "what tragic news?" "This morning they found my former companion dead at the bottom of the cliff below where we lived," she said. I noticed that she called the man her "companion" rather than her husband or spouse, so I conjectured that they had simply lived together, which constituted adultery in the Jewish faith. "Dead?" I replied, not wanting to believe what I was hearing. "Was it an accident or a murder or what?" I asked. "Most likely a suicide," she said softly, stifling a sob.

"I wanted to go back up the mountain and reason with him," I said, tears of sorrow streaming down my face as I hugged Naomi into my shoulder so that she might not hear more of the exchange. "It would not have done any good," Hara said; "he had lost all hope and talked often of jumping off that cliff. His was total despair, and our leaving freed him to pursue what he most wanted, which was freedom from the travails of life."

"I see," I said softly. "Has he had a decent burial with prayers offered to commend his spirit to God?" "No," she said, "the shepherds who found him simply placed him in a crevice in the mountain near where they found him, and covered his body with stones. That's about all that homeless, destitute people here in the mountains can hope for."

"I must go and give him a decent burial," I said. "Then I'll go with you," she said. I struggled to rise with the child still in my arms, and Hara extended her hand and helped me to stand. We started up the mountain, with me carrying Naomi while Hara and I steadied each other by walking arm and arm, both of us weak but committed to the climb.

When we had climbed for a considerable amount of time, we drew close to the base of the cliff, and the circling vultures led us to the site of the make-shift grave. Already odors were permeating the air, and it was not a pleasant sensation. We walked around to the upwind side, and as we stood there, a voice behind us said "There's water coming out of this mountain spring; why not refresh yourselves before you pray?" We turned and discovered Jesus standing there, although we had not seen him when we first arrived at the site. Jesus reached out his arms and took Naomi, and Hara and I found the water, drank deeply, and splashed its refreshing coolness over our now sun-burned faces.

I used my olive wood cup to draw more water which I took to Naomi, and she drank it all. I then asked Jesus to conduct a simple funeral rite, but he deferred to me, noting that it had been impressed on my heart to climb the mountain for such a purpose.

I lifted my eyes to the heavens and prayed earnestly from deep within me. "Lord, God" I said, "we commend the spirit of this man to your care. He had a hard life, and much of the anger and despair he felt was caused by situations and events beyond his control. We ask you that, in your mercy, you forgive and forget the sins that he may have committed, and instead shower him with the forgiveness and love that we believe you offer to all of us. We humbly ask you to welcome this man into eternal life with you, and we thank you and praise you that you are a loving God who offers love, mercy and hope to us all. Amen."

Jesus and Hara repeated the "Amen," and then Hara collapsed at Jesus' feet, clutching his knees and weeping bitterly. I thought that she was merely caught up in the grief of losing her companion, but Jesus immediately knew what was happening, and, handing the child back to me, he gently released her arms from around his legs and knelt down before her. As he steadily gazed at her, she cried out: "I shall surely burn in the fires of hell. I am a sinful woman and unworthy of the mercy and forgiveness that David prayed about."

Jesus spoke softly to her: "You did what you had to do to survive, and later to try to protect your child. God does not judge us harshly when we are subjected to such travail and respond by doing what is necessary. You were forced to give up your virtue. God understands, so now it is time for you to stop being so hard on yourself, and to seek that loving mercy that you want so badly." "I'm not sure God will forgive me," she sobbed.

"I'm not sure you'll forgive you," Jesus said, smiling. "Can you forgive yourself?" he continued. She thought awhile and then nodded. "It will take work, but I'll try my best."

She continued to weep softly, her head facing the ground. "Hara," Jesus said softly, "I forgive you. Hear me: your sins are forgiven. You are now made clean, and you have a bright new life in front of you." She looked up in disbelief. "Forgiven?" she said; "Clean?" She let the words sink in, and then she began to weep again, only her tears were now tears of release and healing and joy. "I believe you," she said softly, and then louder, "I believe you. I am forgiven," she shouted toward the top of the mountain and the sky above it, "I am clean and I am worthwhile. I have a bright new life ahead of me."

She began to laugh. "I am forgiven and clean and worthwhile" she shouted at the top of her lungs. In amazement and awe I had witnessed Jesus healing her and loving her back to life. God's mercy and forgiveness had flowed through him, and she was made whole.

Soon she had totally regained her composure and she softly repeated over and over: "I have a bright new life ahead of me." "Yes," Jesus said softly, "and it will begin by you returning to your master." Hara emitted a piercing scream such as I had never heard before: loud, intense, and full of pain. "I cannot do that," she wailed; "he will violate me again and treat me like dirt and I will be back in the same old situation again."

Her sobbing increased in intensity, and she once again pressed her face to the ground in her despair. Jesus let her cry herself out, and when she had grown silent, Jesus said "I love you both very much, and I wouldn't ask you to do anything that wasn't good for you and the child. It will be different this time, I promise you. You must have faith in me."

"If you wish to be free, you must go back and earn your freedom. At present, you are a fugitive, and subject to all manner of torture and punishment when your master catches you, which someday he will. Better to go back now—better for you, and also for the child. I will go with you. No harm will befall you—I give you my word on that. Because of you, your master and his entire household will eventually repent and return to the God of our fathers. It will take time, and it will not be easy, but the strength I will give you will enable you to stand fast and help bring the kingdom of God to that house. Eventually, your master will be a shining example of righteousness for all of Jerusalem."

Hara sat up and clasped her knees in front of her chest. "I have been defiled in the most grievous of ways," she said; "it will be very difficult for me to go back, and especially to forgive him as I suppose you want me to do." "Yes," Jesus responded, "I want you to forgive him, but for your sake and the sake of the child. Just as I will send the disciples out to preach repentance to a hostile world with only the clothes on their backs, so also I am sending you back to your master's house to preach repentance there. And I know you have the tenacious courage to do what I am asking you to do. You are a strong woman."

I was totally engrossed in the request that Jesus was making. "Be not afraid," Jesus said, "I will go with you at the beginning, and my Spirit will remain with you at all times. Have faith in me—all will surely be well." After a long period of reflection, she finally nodded her hesitant wordless assent, rose, and dropped her black mourning shawl on top of her dead mate's grave. Holding onto my arm, she, I and the child left Jesus and headed down the mountain. When I looked back, Jesus had disappeared.

AMBUSHES

When we rejoined the crowd below on the grassy plain, I became more aware of the presence of a large number of Scribes, Pharisees, Levites, and other religious leaders of the country, all of whom had appeared to investigate this new sensation named "Jesus."

Some of these men had traveled all the way from Jerusalem, which was a multi-day walk for them, and I personally knew a number of them from my role as a Sanhedrin member. In the days ahead, I had many exchanges with these men, most of them unpleasant. While a few of them were open to considering what Jesus had to say, and strove to understand his teachings, most listened to argue and refute his teachings. Although they had historically been arch-enemies of one another as they argued about issues such as life after death, they became united in their intentions to discredit this new evangelist.

They spent long hours with one another perfecting trick questions with which they hoped to trip up Jesus and expose the fallacies of his teachings, and although Jesus was always able to avoid their traps, they continued their plotting with ever-growing intensity. Jesus knew their hearts, and as his patience with their rigidity and intractability ebbed, he became more and more vocal in denouncing them as the hypocrites they were.

Perhaps the thing that troubled them most was the authority with which Jesus spoke, referring often to the Father in heaven and signifying that he was sent by God.

Nor was I spared. They came at me in waves, calling me an "old fool" and an "insane idiot" for listening to a man who appeared to be trying to rewrite the sacred traditions that they held so dear, and with which they held the common people in such moral servitude. They told me that Jesus was a madman, a fake, a magician, an imposter, and that he surely was sent by Satan because of the way he attacked them, the bastions of organized religion in Judea and surely the keepers of the one true faith. They ridiculed me for my absences from the Sanhedrin as I instead roamed the countryside with this romantic fool.

For a while I tried to reason with them and to defend Jesus and his teachings, but as Jesus had already seen, their hearts and minds were closed and they were beyond being converted. Their obstinacy became so great that they denied the miracles that happened before their own eyes, calling such miracles "sleight-of-hand" and "illusions."

But try as I might to convince them to examine what Jesus was saying with an open, seeking mind, they would not do so, but instead, they continued to verbally assail me at every opportunity. They posed the same trick questions to me, and I discovered I was no match for their collective scheming. After a while, I stopped trying to respond to them.

For me, it came down to this: I realized that I was as advanced in Scripture study and knowledge as they were, but that that knowledge did little to feed my interior spiritual life. Instead, Jesus' simple words and teachings made far more sense to me than any ancient scroll, and my spirituality had already grown greatly as a result of his teachings. Reluctantly, I resolved to avoid these saboteurs in the future when possible, and I did.

DISILLUSIONMENT

The rigors of the traveling ministry wore heavily on me, and I became existentially tired and very uninspired. The constant sniping of the religious spies grated on my serenity, and I found myself angrily snapping at them when they confronted me. At times I even let down my guard and broke my promise to myself to treat them lovingly, instead calling them "obstinate fools" and "blind asses" when they refused to consider the validity of Jesus' teachings. I knew that Jesus also had to be on constant alert ahead of their attacks, and the strain on him was very evident to me. The stress they caused him angered me.

The crowds also got on my nerves. It had been idyllic when I could walk alone behind Jesus and the small band of a dozen men, thinking and praying and enjoying my solitude. Now hundreds of people pressed in upon all of us, nearly suffocating us physically, emotionally and spiritually. Some were well-intentioned and sat quietly on the grass in front of Jesus, listening carefully to his words and integrating them into their souls.

But alas, the objectives of others were not so pure. Many were sensationalists who had heard about Jesus and came out to see a show, much like seeing a circus in the Roman arenas. Others wanted money, or a quick fix for their physical problems, or other solutions to their needs, but they were reluctant to actually be engaged in a conversion experience. I saw some people at their best and others at their worst, and the reality that this ministry was not having the universal success I had expected began to sink in.

The most discouraging aspect for me was seeing people who really got the message but would not act upon it, refusing repentance and conversion in favor of their old, sinful ways. I could not understand how this could be so; Jesus' teachings were so simple, so pure, so lofty, so promising and so life-giving, that it baffled me when many heard them and yet turned away. I found myself getting very depressed; my joy had turned to anger.

The other disturbing element was the fact that I had very little contact with Jesus, and certainly no quiet times alone on the mountain with him as I used to, sharing prayer and bread and bravitzka. Without these infusions of encouragement and blessing, I found myself devoid of the energy and commitment I had once had, and the reality of it scared me. I began to seriously question whether or not I was cut out for this mission after all.

I realized that I had to get away by myself for a while and reassess the entire situation. It appeared that we would be staying in this verdant, grassy area of Galilee for some time, so I resolved to retreat to the wilderness in an attempt to regain a balanced perspective.

Shortly before dusk, I walked to the cooking area where I found Judas, to whom we had given the nickname "Thaddeus" to differentiate him from Judas Iscariot. As usual, he was quietly preparing an evening meal for the apostles and disciples, concocting some wonderful dish out of seemingly worthless scraps of food that others might have rejected.

"I'm going away for a few days to pray," I said, and then catching myself in the lie, I corrected myself by saying "actually, I'm going away to see if I can regain my serenity."

"Do you have a little food I could take with me," I continued, "something like a piece of fruit or a small piece of bread?" Thaddeus smiled knowingly. "I wish I could go with you," he said, "because my spirits sink at times as well. But I am needed here, so I will ask you to pray for me to be strengthened also. Come by in the morning, and food for three days will be ready for you. Will that be enough?" "Yes," I said gratefully, "that is exactly how long I will be gone. But I may come by before dawn; will that be too early?" "No," Thaddeus said, "I will make you something tonight, and it will be hanging on that tent pole there in the corner. It will nourish and strengthen you. Drink lots of water."

"I will just be up on the mountain above here," I said, "looking down on this drama as it plays out below me. I will think of you and pray for you whenever I have my food." I then surprised both Thaddeus and myself by embracing him warmly, and he seemed to gratefully sink into my arms much as a needy child would seek its mother's solace. "I am tired and disillusioned too," he said; "pray that I can regain my strength and enthusiasm."

I bid him good evening and found a quiet spot to say my evening prayers and then sleep. But sleep wouldn't come. Shadow seemed restless and ready to be on our way too, so I hefted my carry-bag and went to the cook tent, where I found a large gourd full of liquid, plugged with a hand-carved wooden stopper. In the moonlight I could see a small object resting on top of the gourd, and I realized that it was a feather that Thaddeus must have left for me. I carefully stowed both items in my bag and then allowed Shadow to lead the way. By dawn we had reached the mountaintop and found a private spot for reflection.

DISCERNMENT

As the first tinges of pink appeared in the east, I began to survey my surroundings. Shadow had led me well; we were in the midst of a small amphitheater surrounded by rock outcroppings. When I stood up, I could see the grassy plain below me with the multitudes of people who had slept there overnight. However, when I sat down, I was alone with myself, totally hidden from anyone below me. A small circle of stones had been arranged in the center of the natural depression, perhaps put there by another pilgrim seeking strength and enlightenment. I wondered if he had found what he sought.

I heard a trickling sound behind me and I realized that there was a small spring emanating from the side of the mountain. I drank heartily from it, and then sat down on a stone above it from whence I could see the sunrise over Lake Galilee. Once again, the show of God's beauty was breath-taking, and I prayed aloud in thanksgiving for being able to see this sight while most of the rest of the world was still asleep. The morning fishing boats looked like dots on the surface of the water, and I wondered if Peter missed his fishing.

Finally the sun rose and I knew that I had to begin my vigil of waiting for enlightenment about what I should be doing in view of my discouragement and disenchantment. I got down off of the rock and entered into the small prayer circle of stones, where I sat down on the already warm ground. My intention was to sit there for as long as it took

God to inspire my heart and show me what I should do in the future. I was in for a long wait.

By mid-morning the sun was beating down mercilessly, and I wondered why Shadow hadn't led me to a different place, a place with shade. I sat on the ground, already questioning why I had wanted to come away to such a lonely place. While I waited for the inspiration that didn't materialize, I watched a few insects apparently wandering aimlessly in the arid soil, and while they appeared to not have a reason for being nor a destination, I knew that they were part of a bigger plan and indeed had a purpose. I left the circle to get water several times as the morning wore on. I was extremely uncomfortable and disillusioned about my enforced solitude.

A noon meal of Jude Thaddeus' concoction heartened me a bit; it was a thick, gruel-like liquid which was filling and delicious. I forced myself to remain in the circle of stones, and by mid-afternoon I was truly suffering greatly from the heat and dehydration, despite frequent drinks of the cool spring water. My thoughts drifted to the beggars in the streets of Jerusalem. A family member or two would take them to their begging spot and then leave them for the day, often with nothing more than a small gourd of water. I wondered how the armless ones managed to drink. I wondered how the crippled managed to walk to a place to relieve themselves. I wondered how any of them tolerated the intense heat.

I was horrified to imagine how it must be to sit in the sun all day, six days a week, and have no hope of one's condition ever improving—how it must be to hope for a few coins from passers-by to give to one's family to buy a few scraps of food for all. I became light-headed from the heat and depressed by my realizations about the poor beggars.

Throughout the afternoon, I had kept waiting for Jesus to appear to console me, hearten me, strengthen me, affirm me, and bless me, but he did not appear. I remained alone.

As the shadows lengthened, I left the circle and walked to a rock where I could sit down and watch the spectacle on the grassy plain below. Hundreds of people were encamped there, all of them magnetized by the teaching and healing of Jesus. While I had been impatient that they seemed slow or even unwilling to grasp his teachings and change accordingly, I began to realize that their primary reason for being there was to have their suffering eased, be it physical, emotional or spiritual. They wanted a less-burdensome, freer, more fulfilling life. Suddenly my aversion to their pushing and shoving to get near Jesus, their rudeness, and their insistent clamoring for healing vanished, and in its place, a strong identification with them took over my soul. They only wanted what I wanted from Jesus, which was consolation, encouragement, strength, affirmation, love, and blessing.

I realized that they were just like me, fellow sojourners! I resolved to suspend my judgments and instead view them as God's beloved, and to treat them accordingly. I further realized that I had felt superior to these people, given my privileged relationship with Jesus, and that this superiority complex must be replaced with true compassion.

I clearly perceived another kind of suffering from which they wanted relief, the pain of being suppressed and oppressed by the Romans. They eagerly looked forward to the Messiah who would lead them to triumph over Rome, and many of them hoped that Jesus might be that leader. I became far more empathetic to their wants, needs, and aspirations.

I also became more understanding about why many of them were resistant to Jesus' message and turned away to return home, even after the miraculous healings they were experiencing. Their suffering at the hands of the Romans was so intense, and their hatred so deep, that any message based on forgiveness of your enemies and love for those who hate you was anathema and completely unpalatable. When it became obvious that Jesus had no intentions of being a rebel and a military leader who would reclaim all of Israel by force, many of them rejected his message as unrealistic and impossible to practice. For the first time, I saw with great clarity that even the love Jesus had for them and showed them in countless ways would probably not be enough to persuade them to change. My hope for a complete conversion of the entire populace was idealistic and unrealizable.

As it grew dark, I returned to my circle and reclined on the ground. It was sobering for me to discover that Jesus' mission would not be the wholesale success that I had hoped it would be. And with the powerful religious leaders growing more openly opposed to his teachings, it might well be that, after the initial sensationalism wore off, we would be left with only a small percentage of the people willing to embrace Jesus' teaching.

I eventually fell into a fitful sleep, and I had the sensation that bugs were crawling on me throughout the night. I kept being awakened by the howls of predators and the screams of their prey as life and death played out in split-second encounters in the dark. I would have been too scared to remain in the spot if it were not for Shadow's presence.

Instead, I would have hurried away in the dark, no doubt taking a serious fall in the process.

In the absolute darkness during the middle of the night, Shadow stirred and I sat bolt upright, conscious that someone was looking at me. A ghostly figure loomed just outside the periphery of the stone circle, and I hoped that it was Jesus, but it was not. Waves of fear washed over me. I was paralyzed, unable to move or flee. The figure began speaking to me, and while the voice was familiar, I didn't recognize it at first.

"Do not lose heart," the voice said, "for you have chosen the right path. I should have followed your example, but I was too proud and too sinful." I suddenly realized that it was my father speaking to me. He continued: "I am in a place of desolation and torment, and I don't know if I will ever be able to leave from here. Do not falter but rather have faith in Jesus' calling. Take heart and be strong. Pray for me, oh please pray for me."

The figure disappeared. At first I thought I must have dreamt the whole encounter, but then I realized that I was sitting up and fully awake. So I questioned whether or not I had imagined the whole encounter, but Shadow's stirring convinced me that the entire event had been real. I reviewed my father's words over and over again throughout the rest of the night. "Take heart, you have chosen the right path, trust Jesus fully, pray for me."

I stayed sitting, unable to sleep, hearing the screams of seized prey and realizing that life can be snuffed out in an instant, without us ever suspecting that death is imminent. What was playing out on the grassy plain below me was the struggle between spiritual life and death, and I realized most of the participants weren't even aware of the unfolding drama.

Dawn of the second day began to break in the east, with a painter's palette of pinks, oranges, purples and other subtle hues too intermingled and subtle to categorize. I sat on the stone overlooking the valley and recited my morning prayers, which somehow seemed more meaningful and intense than usual. I knew it would be a memorable day.

I was inspired with an idea that I decided to act upon. Just before sunrise, I retrieved my two olive-wood plates and two cups from my carry-bag. I filled both of the cups with water and placed them near the center of the stone circle. I placed the plates there also; on one I placed the feather Jude Thaddeus had given me, and the other one I left empty, symbolizing the beggar's tin cup or plate upon which hoped-for alms would be placed.

As the sun broke in the East above Lake Galilee, I drank heartily at the spring and then entered the circle, resolved to sit there until sunset in a reenactment of a street beggar's day in Jerusalem. I would experience what they experience and feel what they feel.

I was very tired from lack of sleep during the previous night, so I laid down in the circle and fell asleep. At some point I stirred and accidentally knocked over one of the cups of water; that left only one cup for the twelve hours I would spend in the circle. At first I was angry at myself for my clumsiness, but then I realized that this was the type of thing that could have easily happened to a paralyzed beggar, who would then sit in the sun all day without any water. I was already restless and uncomfortable, and a wave of negative thoughts filled my mind. Perhaps this was a foolish idea and I should leave the circle.

As the sun grew higher and hotter, I began to suffer greatly. I hoarded my last cup of water, not wanting to use it up too early in the day, and I moved it far away from me so I would not spill it also. I was hot, dehydrated and spiritless, and I questioned my decision.

As the day wore on, I became more and more empathetic with the suffering of the street beggars, and in fact with all of the poor who experienced illness and deprivation in their lives. I realized that these were the people to whom Jesus was ministering. Although I wore my prayer shawl to protect my head from the sun, I was nevertheless getting boiled by the bright sun and unmerciful heat, and I was truly miserable. I kept watching the sun, trying to urge it to speed up its pace toward the horizon, but the day seemed to never end.

At the height of the afternoon sun and heat, I began to experience sunstroke and I started hallucinating, imagining all manner of vultures and demons ready to prey upon me. The only thing that kept me at all calm was the reassuring presence of Shadow at my side.

Finally the sun touched the top of the mountains west of my position, and in a few minutes it had set. I had never had a more trying day in my life, and I realized that this was "everyday" for the beggars, and that also, they could never look forward to any end to their pitiful existence. I tried to imagine what it was like sitting in the dry dung on the edge of the road for six days each week, and the feeling of rejection, worthlessness and hopelessness these beggars must feel when almost everyone passing by looked the other way, refusing to give them even a few coppers as a sign of caring and support.

It was a very profound day, yielding much insight about the plight of those less fortunate than myself, and also about the affirmation, encouragement and healing Jesus offered. My heart was overflowing with compassion for these unfortunate people, and I resolved to never again walk by them without sitting on the ground for a few moments or more next to them, connecting with them, blessing them, and giving them the love of Jesus.

When the sun had totally disappeared, I ended my vigil in the circle and proceeded to the spring, where I let the cold water run over me for a very long time. It felt life-saving. My lips were cracked and my face raw with sunburn, and I realized that I could have died in the unbearable heat. How did these poor beggars stand such daily torment?

I sat on the rocky bluff of the mountain, once again looking down on the multitude gathered around Jesus, seeking temporal relief from their illnesses, discouragement, and even near-starvation. While Jesus was bringing a profoundly spiritual message as well, most of these people were too caught up in their neediness to fully grasp and embrace it.

I said my evening prayers, thanking God for all of the insights I had received, despite or perhaps because of the extreme physical suffering I had endured during the day. As darkness fell, I earnestly wanted to rest and sleep, but I had carelessly not removed my clothes when I got under the refreshing water, and now my wet garments were another source of discomfort as the surprisingly cool evening air sent a chill over my entire body. I knew I faced a long, sleepless night, so I sat and prayed that more insights might come.

ENLIGHTENMENT

I spent the night shivering in the cold, and whereas I had suffered from the sun's heat during the previous day, I now yearned for its warming rays. Finally, as the first tinges of pink appeared in the sky over the east shore of Lake Galilee, I was suddenly filled with an overwhelming sense of gratitude to God for the sun, for food, for clothing, for life, for everything that I had previously taken for granted. I resolved to stop being resentful about things that formerly bothered me: the heat, the cold, the food, or anything else. As the sun rose and began to dry my damp clothes, my spirits were lifted and I felt real joy.

The joy surprised me, and I realized that I had been lacking it for some time. In fact, I realized that I had come to the mountain for these three days to examine my heart and to attempt to identify why I had become disillusioned, and what I should do about it. It came to me during my extended morning prayers that the key to regaining what I had lost was to review my life and identify when I was happiest. In that would be my answer.

Identifying that time was not hard to do. I realized that I was most fulfilled when I was walking alone behind Jesus and the apostles and one of them would drop back to talk to me. Sometimes they were just being sociable, but at other times they were seeking understanding, encouragement or a way out of any disillusionment that they were feeling. I saw that instead I had gotten caught up in trying to minister to the crowds, and that such activity was only tiring and discouraging me. This insight was vital to adjusting my life.

At mid-morning I finished the tasty gruel-like food that Thaddeus had prepared for me. At the same time, I kept looking at the feather sitting in my dish inside the circle. Despite some strong breezes during the night, it had not blown away. It was a beautiful, multi-colored feather, perfect in every respect. I wondered what Judas Thaddeus had in mind when he left it for me along with my food. Then it hit me, and I knew.

In the middle of his own disillusionment, he wanted me to know that he was with me in spirit here on this mountaintop, that we were kindred souls, and that I had his regard and support. I now visualized him already peeling the vegetables for the late-day meal, and I sent him love and affection while praying that his time of struggle would pass by quickly.

And with my prayer, the final insight came. I was not called by Jesus to minister to the crowds, but rather to the apostles themselves. In the middle of the stressful busy-ness, Jesus did not always have time or availability to attend to their psychic wounds, and he was counting on me to do so. But I, distracted, had drifted away from my assigned task!

I was elated to think about returning to what I did best: being quietly present and available for these men, whom I loved, when they needed solace and encouragement.

I stayed in the shade all day, drinking copious amounts of the cool spring water and praying that I would be able to stay focused on my true vocation. I now saw my path clearly.

At dusk I headed down the mountain and directly to the cooking tent.

As I expected, Judas Thaddeus was there, busily preparing yet another meal for Jesus and the apostles. When he saw me coming, he dropped what he was doing, ran to greet me, and embraced me warmly. "Well, how was it Elder David?" he queried, surprising me with the directness and immediacy of his question. Still in his embrace, I looked him in the eyes and I said "it was a powerful experience, filled with suffering and insights and also great joy. Parts of me died on the mountain and better parts of me were born anew."

He nodded his head understandingly. "My spirit was with you," he confided, "and I fasted for the entire three days so that God might work mightily in your heart." The news of his fasting hit me hard; I got emotional, and began sobbing in his arms. I had come to love this gentle, humble man, and it was just like him to offer up his own self for another.

"I have a new appreciation for the plight of the poor, and especially of beggars," I said, "and I have a clear vision of the loving service I must provide, often devoid of the notice of Jesus. Quiet, loving service such as that which you provide to us every day." At this point, it was Judas Thaddeus' turn to cry. "The hardest part," he said, "is in not seeing Jesus very much. But I know he loves me and appreciates my efforts, and that will have to suffice."

We walked back to the cook tent and removing my cloak, I began helping Jude Thaddeus peel vegetables and prepare the meal. He seemed surprised, and protested loudly: "You don't have to do this menial work, David" he said. "Oh, but I want to," I replied; "if service is what we're called to provide, let's support one another and provide it together."

THE BRIEFING

A few days later, Shadow again roused me in the middle of the night, and grabbing my carry-bag, I proceeded to follow him up the mountain. As I expected, Jesus was already there, quietly praying and mediating in the chilly pre-dawn air. Seeing me, he arose, embraced me warmly, and said "Shalom, Elder David, I am happy to see you." "Yes," I said, "it's been quite a while since we have connected, but I have come to see that that is the way it must be as you get ever more deeply involved in your work. It was hard on me for a while, but now I am content to stay in the background and serve the apostles."

"Your time on the mountain was well spent," Jesus said, "and you have discerned well. You are correct in realizing that the way you can serve me best is to keep my apostles encouraged, motivated and insightful. I have entrusted you with this special mission."

Jesus gestured toward my carry-bag and asked for my olive-wood plate, which he handed back half-full of plain yet tasty pastries, and then he asked for my cup, which he filled with steaming bravitzka. "This will be a memorable day for us," Jesus said, "and from now on I will need your love and support more than ever. I know that I already have those things and that your heart overflows with love, and I feed on that knowledge, but I also know that you occasionally have doubts, and that you struggle with how best to proceed. Just know that, as your father told you, you have chosen the right path." I exhaled loudly; "I'm sorry I need reassurance at times, but that's just how I am," I said.

"You're doing fine," Jesus said, "and you are a blessing to me. Get enough rest, don't overdo, and remember that the best service you can provide is to be a prayerful witness and a compassionate loving source of strength that the apostles can admire and emulate. You'll never know how much your gentle affirmation of Jude Thaddeus has lifted his spirits, and you can provide that same encouragement to the rest of the men at all times."

"Why will this be a memorable day?" I asked. "I am the source of the rise and fall of many," Jesus replied. "I am asking people to look deeply into their hearts to discover what's really there, and I am asking them to reexamine their basic beliefs and change those beliefs as needed. Also, I am not bringing the message that many of them had hoped to hear, and some will find it difficult to embrace such a divergent viewpoint."

We both grew silent as we watched the first pink tinges appear over the ridge above the east shore of Lake Galilee. I never tired of this panoramic reminder of God's power and beauty, and it inspired me to want to never leave this idyllic setting on the mountaintop. However, Jesus had a different agenda, and helping me to my feet, he proceeded to lead us back down the mountainside. Sensing my reluctance to end our time together on the summit, Jesus said "You know, peeling vegetables is also praying when done with the right intention." I looked at him and saw the twinkle in his eyes, and I knew that he understood that restful solitude was more appealing to me than busy, inter-personal engagement. "You have formed your life into a healthy blend of prayer, contemplation, and action," he concluded, "and that mixture will continue to serve both you and I well."

THE CHALLENGE

As dawn broke, we looked down at the scene below us. Hundreds of people were gathered in small groups, some with small tents or cloth shelters, but most with just their own clothing to protect them. Many were still sleeping, while here and there a small fire indicated that some people were up and combating the chill while also preparing breakfast. It was an incredible sight, the likes of which had probably not been seen since the Israelites camped in the desert for forty years before entering this beautiful land.

Up until now, Jesus had mostly moved between relatively small groups of people, healing the sick and expelling demons while also sharing his teachings when possible. I sensed that today might be different, and that Jesus' approach to his work might change.

It promised to be one of the most beautiful days possible in this lush, verdant valley, with bright sunshine to liven the people accompanied by a gentle breeze to cool them. The sun had not fully risen yet as we reached the cook tent, where Jesus sought out Peter, Andrew and James, took them aside, and began talking earnestly to them. They in turn gathered the rest of the apostles and conveyed Jesus' wishes. At mid-morning, the apostles began gathering the people on a large, grassy slope that extended from the top of the mountain all the way to Lake Galilee. The terrain formed a natural amphitheater with good acoustics, and a small cluster of boulders near the summit provided a spot from which Jesus could be seen and heard as he addressed the crowd. The stage was set.

SHOCKING NEWS

Jesus had spent many weeks on the Plains of Gennesaret, interspersed with occasional trips into nearby Capernaum, where he preached in the temple on the Sabbath. Crowds overflowed out of the small building and onto the adjacent courtyard. The people loved to hear Jesus teach; he spoke with authority, they said, unlike the Scribes who normally conducted the worship services. Of course, the Scribes greatly resented this comparison.

The apostles appreciated these times, because it gave them a respite to relax a bit and spend time with their families. Inevitably, however, Jesus returned to the countryside where he healed illnesses, expelled demons, and alleviated other travails of the people.

Consequently, on this morning there were several thousand people clustered around him in this idyllic setting. Most of them hoped that Jesus would emerge as the triumphant Messiah who would overthrow the Romans and return Israel to its former glory. They also longed for more prosperous times—times of free-flowing milk and honey, when they would be spared from their everyday toils and be able to live a life of ease and luxury.

On this day, they would have that hope crushed, and many would leave him as a result. Jesus sat on a large boulder and gestured to me to sit on a smaller one slightly behind him and to his right, my usual place when I was with him. All eyes were focused on him.

Jesus began to speak with disappointing news for the crowd. "Blessed are the poor, the kingdom of God is yours. Happy are you who are hungry now; you will be filled. Happy are you who weep, happy are you when people hate you, reject you, insult you, and say that you are evil, all because of me. Be glad when that happens and dance for joy, because a great reward awaits you in heaven." "How can you dance for joy on an empty stomach?" a heckler cried out, to which Jesus replied: "How terrible for you who are rich now, for you have had your easy life. How terrible for you who are full now, you will go hungry! How terrible for you who laugh now, for you will mourn and weep."

The heckler yelled back: "You have the power to feed thousands and raise the dead. Lead us against the Romans, so we can reclaim our heritage." Jesus replied: "Love your enemies, do good to those who hate you, bless those who curse you, and pray for those who mistreat you. Do not judge others, and God will not judge you; do not condemn others, and God will not condemn you; forgive others, and God will forgive you."

At this the man got up, gathered his family members, and left the site. Others followed and before long, several hundred people were seen departing. Jesus seemed saddened by this, but continued to teach the remaining people. He then returned to Capernaum. There was a Roman centurion there who had a gravely ill servant. Jesus was asked to heal him and he headed for the centurion's home. The centurion sent word that Jesus need not come in person but only say the word and his servant would be healed. Jesus expressed amazement at the man's faith, said the word, and the servant got well at that moment.

NO REST

For the next several months, Jesus concentrated most of his ministry within a relatively small area around Capernaum, a bustling village which was the center of fishing and agriculture activities. Jesus rarely went much farther from Capernaum than a day's walking distance. Instead people came to him from all over, seeking healing, forgiveness of their sins, freedom from demons, or favors for other family members or friends.

His time was spent teaching and healing, and he found it more and more difficult to get away by himself for meditation, prayer and rest. Once, when he was exhausted, he bade the apostles to take him across the lake in a boat to get away for a while, but the people hurried around the north end of the lake and were waiting for him when he landed on the other side. The pressure on him was incredible, and he often showed signs of fatigue.

One time he was so weary that he fell asleep in Peter's boat and was sleeping through a life-threatening storm that had arisen; the apostles were terrified and woke him out of a deep slumber to calm the waves, which he did. There were successes and failures in the ministry, times of great joy and times of disappointment. Some he healed with just his gentle touch. Others he challenged to dig deep into their psyche for the faith in him and his power that would enable them to be healed. He forgave harlots and ate with other known sinners, and all were touched by him and moved to conversion. He walked the fields and taught the crowds using examples from nature. It was a very unusual ministry.

The apostles perceived themselves to be little more than facilitators of Jesus' work, so one day they were surprised when Jesus called them together and commissioned them to pair up and go out into the countryside themselves. He gave them specific instructions on what to wear and how to proceed and he promised to empower them with the same power he had to cure the sick, cast out demons, and perform other miracles like he did. The apostles were stunned, and also wary about the assignment, but they obeyed and went out to all of the villages, and they were amazed at the miracles they performed in his name.

When they returned, they enthusiastically reported the successes they had had as they saw many wonders happen when they invoked the name of Jesus. They began to recount what had happened, but the crowds again started to press in, so Jesus proposed that they escape to Bethsaida for a respite and a debriefing. However, the crowds followed them there, too, so he welcomed them, told them about the Kingdom of God, and healed them.

Toward nightfall, the apostles urged Jesus to send the people away so that they might find food and lodging for the night, but there were no signs of the large crowd dispersing. The apostles then offered to go into a nearby village to find food, but Jesus responded by asking if they themselves had any food. "Five loaves and two fishes," they responded, "but what is that among so many?" Jesus instructed them to have the people be seated in groups of fifty, and taking food in his hands, he thanked God for it, broke it, and bade the apostles distribute it among the people, five thousand men in number. All ate and were satisfied, and the apostles collected twelve baskets of leftover food. All were amazed.

PASSOVER

Jesus was accustomed to returning to Jerusalem each year for Passover, so as the signs of Spring appeared, he began working his way southward through Galilee toward Samaria. Traveling through Magdala, we again skirted Nazareth and Tiberias and instead stayed in more remote places. Nevertheless, there were still opportunities for Jesus to teach the people who followed him and to work miracles among those we met needing healing.

While still in Galilee, Jesus went up a mountain one day, taking only Peter, James, and John with him. When they came back, we knew from the looks on their faces that something momentous had happened, but they could only tell us that they had seen Jesus in all of his glory and majesty, and that he surely was the chosen one of God.

There were still a large number of disciples with us, and Jesus chose seventy-two of them and sent them out to all of the towns and villages we would be passing through, with instructions similar to the ones he had given the apostles previously. The seventy-two went forth in faith, and they later returned, full of joy about their power over demons.

When the group entered Samaria, one town refused it entrance because the people knew Jesus and the apostles were Jews heading for Jerusalem. The apostles wanted retribution, but Jesus replied that instead they'd go on to another more welcoming town to stay. By and by they entered Judea and headed for the home of Mary, Martha, and Lazarus in Bethany.

HARA'S RETURN

As we traveled closer to Jerusalem, the number of those following Jesus was reduced to the apostles and a few of the most faithful men and women disciples. We stopped for the night outside of Bethany, in a pastoral setting at the edge of a beautiful olive grove.

Early the next morning, long before daybreak, I became conscious of Shadow stirring, so I rose quickly, reached for my carry bag, and followed Shadow up to the top of the mountain. Jesus was there, deep in prayer, and I sat down and waited respectfully for him to complete his prayers. When he did, he gestured for me to pass him my olive-wood cup and plate. He handed me back a full cup of steaming bravitzka, a whole roll, and some fresh fruit, while he also partook of the same wonderful breakfast.

"Shalom," he said. "This day salvation will come to a house of sin and abomination in Jerusalem. In a short while I will go there with Hara. I want you to come along as well."

Shortly after sunrise, we headed down the mountain path, and near the bottom, Hara and Naomi were already waiting for us. Hara was still weak from the near-starvation she had suffered earlier, so I again happily offered to carry Naomi, who snuggled into my arms and immediately fell back to sleep, while Hara held onto the arm of Jesus. She was remarkably calm and she even appeared strong in her resolve to do Jesus' bidding, no matter how difficult it might prove to be. We entered the city through the East Gate.

By mid-morning we had entered a section of Jerusalem where the wealthiest citizens resided, and soon we came to the entrance of a very impressive home. We entered the outside portico, where a man-servant challenged us as to our purpose in being there. When he looked at Hara, a brief flash of recognition crossed his face, but he said nothing.

"Please tell your master that the Rabbi wishes to speak with him," Jesus said. "We are not used to receiving uninvited guests," the servant said brusquely, "what is it that I should tell him you want." "Tell him that we bring salvation," Jesus said; "that should be enough for him to see us." The servant snickered loudly and retreated through the door.

After an extended wait, Masma, Hara's owner, appeared in the courtyard, where he sized up the situation quickly. "Oh," he said, "the slut has returned, and with a new mate."

"She has never been a slut," Jesus said, "but only an innocent child whom you bought so as to continually violate and debase her." The man turned bright red and began to rush at Jesus, his arm raised and his fist clenched. I stepped between them, but he roughly shoved me aside and was about to hit Jesus when he encountered Jesus' calm, steady gaze, strong and utterly fearless. He stopped, fist still clenched in mid-air, and then slowly lowered his arm. "Nobody talks to me like that in my own household," he said.

"What other lies has she told you?", he continued, nodding toward Hara. "She has told me nothing," Jesus responded, "I already know everything that occurred." "I don't believe you," Masma said; "leave her and depart from my home. You are not welcome here."

Jesus did not move, and Masma was about to summon his servants to expel Jesus forcibly when Jesus again spoke. "I saw you murder the slave boy under the sycamore tree when he resisted your carnal advances," Jesus said. "I did no such..." Masma started to say, and then stopped in mid-sentence. Something about Jesus' look alerted him to the fact that denial would do him no good. "Nobody was supposed to know about that," Masma said quietly.

"I know your heart and everything that's in it," Jesus said, "and it's black and rotten in there. You will surely burn in Gahanna for eternity if you do not change your ways."

Masma was silent for a while, and after he regained his composure, he once again tried to become master of the situation. "Who does the little bastard belong to," he asked, "the slave she ran off with, or someone else, or even you? Tell me prophet, I want to know."

Hara spoke for the first time, bravely and assertively: "It is yours, my master Masma, the girl is your child. Her name is Naomi." Masma was flabbergasted. "Then why did you run away?", he asked incredulously. "Because I did not want her to suffer the same shame and indignity that I have suffered," Hara responded. "You treated me like a whore and tried to destroy my self-esteem, and I did not want her to suffer the same cruel fate. Knowing that she would be raped while still a child was more than I could bear to face. I was willing to risk running away in the hope that I could give her a respectable life."

"But it didn't work out, did it?' Masma said sarcastically. "I am here of my own free will," she replied, "but I will never again let you treat me as you treated me in the past."

"And what if I do?", Masma asked sarcastically, again trying to regain control of the situation. "I don't know," Hara said, "I hope it never comes to having to decide."

"My wife has died since you were here," Masma said; "perhaps we could have a more amicable relationship." "Not as long as you are brutally forcing your carnal attentions on young boys and girls in the same household," Hara said; "I couldn't abide such actions."

Jesus reentered the conversation. "Your wife died of a broken heart," Jesus said, "because of the shame she felt about what she knew was going on. She no longer wanted to live in such a sin-filled environment. Hara doesn't either," he added; "no one does."

Masma became thoughtful. "Tell me again about Gahanna," he said. "Gahanna is eternal torment," Jesus said, "where those acting contrary to the ways of God will suffer forever, while the humble and pure of spirit will exist eternally in heaven with the Lord."

"I'm not committing to anything," Masma said, "but tell me what you would have me do to avoid such punishment." "First," Jesus said, "think of it as gaining eternal life rather than just avoiding punishment." Masma nodded. "Repent of your evil ways. Get down on your knees and pray every day for God to forgive you, which he surely will. Treat Hara and Naomi with dignity and respect. Become an example of virtue that all can respect. And finally, court Hara and try to earn her hand as your new wife. It will take time, and you must abstain from all carnal pleasure until then, but it may come to pass."

Hara and I both gasped in surprise at Jesus' words, but Hara didn't speak up to refute the possibility of such an occurrence. Meanwhile, Masma sank onto a nearby bench and began to sob. "I just want to love and be loved," he sobbed, "and I've never found out how to make it work. I have gone about it in all of the wrong ways, and I'm miserable. I've always admired your dignity and your strength, Hara" Masma said. "Could what he's suggesting ever happen? Would you consider trying to make such a thing occur?"

"I need to be convinced that you have truly repented," she responded. "What I most want is a safe, nurturing environment for our daughter. I will constantly watch out to make sure she is receiving that. I need also to work at forgiving you. I have suffered greatly at your hands and it will take time for the wounds to heal. But I am willing to try."

"I can command you to become my wife or else die," Masma said, partially talking to himself, "but I can see that that would never work. I don't know how to court anybody," he continued, "but I am asking you in all humility if you will show me how." Hara didn't respond, but instead shifted the topic. "This house must become a shining example of fidelity to the Lord of Israel. This man, Jesus of Nazareth, knows the way to live forever, and from this day forward, this home must believe in his way and support his ministry."

Masma slid off the bench and knelt at her feet. "You have my word that such will be so." She took his hand and helped him to his feet. Masma reached out his arms to take Naomi, and she easily slid into his embrace. "Let's start Masma," Hara said smiling, "let's start." Jesus blessed the three of them, and then he and I left them together and reentered the sunlit street.

JOSHUA

We strolled back through the streets of Jerusalem, heading for the East Gate. Jesus seemed to be in no particular hurry, and we enjoyed the sights and sounds of the bustling city as we walked along. As I thought about the events of the morning, I was again overwhelmed with love for this wonderful man, and I decided to tell him. "I love you, Jesus," I said, "my heart is overflowing with love for you." "I love you too, David," he responded, "and your love and constancy strengthen me to keep going in this ministry."

We walked a bit further, and since we were both in good humor, I decided to extend the conversation further. "You never cease to amaze me," I said; "I never would have guessed how well that encounter with Masma went. You seem to have a knack to know exactly how to manage each situation to effect a positive outcome." "Not always," Jesus replied; "there are times when people don't want to be happy and to be saved, such as the man on the mountain who gave up Hara and Naomi and then gave up his life as well."

I nodded. "Will Hara and Masma make it?" I asked. "Yes, but it will take longer than Masma would hope. Masma is a good man who did a lot of bad things. He learned such evil behavior from his father, and it is all he has ever known. He will have to start from scratch to learn to be virtuous, but Hara is the perfect person to teach him, and she will.

"The child is the key," Jesus continued; "Masma is childless and very much wants to love a child and be loved by it. Naomi will be the reason the story will have a happy ending."

As we came around a corner, a weak voice from the side of the road said "Alms, for the poor, you men, please, alms for the poor." I looked and saw a nearly lifeless old man by the side of the street, sitting amidst the camel and donkey dung, devoid of both legs.

Jesus again surprised me by sitting down next to him, and I soon sat down as well. "Good morning, Joshua, and how are you today?", Jesus said, apparently not noticing the filthy area in which he was sitting. A quick look of surprise crossed the man's face, but after a moment he replied in a weak voice: "I am sick and hungry," he said. "And how is it that you know my name? No other passer-by cares about me or knows my name."

"You are neither sick nor hungry," Jesus said matter-of-factly, "but you surely are clever. By digging deep depressions in the dirt, you can kneel down so your legs don't show and so that people will believe you are legless. And the 'old man' disguise is done perfectly. Probably no one has ever guessed you are much younger and very successful at begging."

I looked at Joshua's begging cup, which contained only a few pence, and wondered what Jesus was driving at with his words. I also expected Joshua to become angry about being found-out, but instead he became very melancholy. "This ruse is all that I know how to do," he said, "and it is all that I have left in life." "Not true," Jesus countered, "you are indeed gifted and have much to offer if you want to. Tell me your story from the start."

"It seems that you already know all about me," Joshua countered stubbornly. "I do know all about you," Jesus replied, "but you don't know all about you, so tell me your story."

Joshua became noticeably sad, even melancholy. "I was born into a wealthy family," he said, eyes downcast, "and I realized from an early age that someday when my father died, I too would be rich. So I never applied myself when the rabbis tried to teach me, and I never had any interest in learning a trade. When my father died, I inherited large tracts of land and a large sum of money. I got greedy and wanted even more so I began gambling, and eventually I lost everything. Not knowing any other way to make a living, I devised this beggar deception and now it is all that I have. My life is empty and meaningless."

"You are a 'taker'," Jesus said. I silently marveled at how Jesus knew just what to say, and who he could challenge and who he couldn't, and who was teachable and who wasn't. Joshua was apparently open and teachable. "You are a 'taker'," Jesus repeated, "and takers are never happy. They are always on the look-out for how they can get something from other people without earning it. For them, enough is never enough."

"I've always thought that accumulating a lot of wealth would bring happiness," Joshua said, "even if it was at the expense of others. My father made his fortune by working his servants and slaves until they literally died where they dropped. Then he would buy more servants and slaves and repeat the process. It's all that I've ever known."

" 'Givers' are the people who are truly happy," Jesus said. "They can give everything they have away, and still be abundantly happy. They know that their Father in heaven will bless them abundantly for their generosity. They do not need any earthly treasures."

Joshua became even more downcast. "I only want to be abundantly happy," he said sorrowfully, "but I don't know how to go about it." "Come and follow me," Jesus said, and you will lack for nothing that is truly important. Furthermore, you will become empowered to heal the lame, the blind, the deaf, the demonized, the lost and unhappy."

"Do you mean come with you right now?" Joshua asked. "Yes," Jesus said, "right now."

Joshua suddenly sprang to his feet, casting aside the robes that had concealed his legs. He shook the powder out of his hair and beard, and wiped off the fake lines he had painted onto his face. We suddenly saw the 30-year-old man under the disguise.

"Come with me first," Joshua said, "and then I will come and follow you." Jesus nodded, and we followed Joshua as he hurried through the streets.

We soon came upon another legless old beggar, sitting alongside the road. "This was my competition," Joshua said; "I got the idea for my disguise from him. We have competed for the same alms. The difference is that he really is old and legless, hungry and sick."

Joshua wrapped his robes around the beggar, and reaching under his tunic, Joshua produced a large purse full of gold coins. "This is all that I have in the world," he said to Jesus and me, "and I now give it willingly to this tired, ailing old man. It will bring him some comfort and solace in his declining years, and I no longer have any need for it."

"Joshua the Giver!" Jesus exclaimed. "This day you have found salvation," Jesus added, beaming with joy. "You have the courage of Joshua, your namesake, and your generosity will be rewarded in heaven. Welcome to our group. Let us be on our way."

BETHANY

It was the first time I had visited Bethany, and I liked it immediately. By now our traveling group had shrunk to Jesus, the twelve apostles, a few disciples, a few of the most loyal women, and me. The home of Jesus' friends was very large, and the women in the group were given sleeping quarters inside, while the rest of us slept and ate on the spacious shaded patios surrounding the main house. The meals were warm and healthful.

Jesus needed badly to rest, which he did. The color came back into his complexion, the dark circles under his eyes lessened in severity, and he was actually light and joyful. He seemed to especially enjoy all of the signs of spring, and he looked at the flowers often.

We went into the temple each day to pray, and he would teach the people who amassed around him on the outer terrace. He would repeatedly warn them to not be like the Scribes and Pharisees, despite the fact that he knew there were spies in the crowd who recounted everything he said to the religious authorities. He frequently entered into discussions with some of the leaders; some were sincere and were seeking a closer relationship with God, while others wanted nothing more than to trap and embarrass him.

Joshua stayed with us at all times, and he was always happy. He developed into a great practical joker, and there was always laughter wherever Joshua was. I realized that we had become quite a somber group, and Joshua's joy was a welcome breath of fresh air.

INCREASED OPPOSITION

Whenever we entered Jerusalem to worship in the temple, I was sought out by members of the Sanhedrin whom I had known for many years. All were amazed that I had taken leave of my home and my exalted position in the governing body of Israel to follow an itinerant rabbi who seemed to most prefer being in the wilderness of Galilee.

Some of these leaders approached me with sincerity and truly seemed to want to more fully understand who Jesus was, what his teachings were, and what his intentions were. Others, however, accosted me and accused me of being a misguided fool, and even a traitor to the one covenanted faith of our fathers. It seemed that I always had to be on guard, but I tried to respond to everyone alike with charity and equanimity. Nevertheless I was surprised at how stressful it was to be in Jerusalem, and I too preferred Galilee.

Jesus also was constantly assailed by the religious leaders, and I could tell that it wore on him greatly. However, I marveled at his complete knowledge of the sacred writings and his consummate skill as a debater. I never once saw him bested by the various traps laid for him by means of the questions the religious leaders had worked so hard to formulate.

This obstinacy frustrated Jesus and myself; it seemed that the religious leaders should have wanted the same thing that Jesus wanted, which was a growing closeness to the Father, but instead they could not see past their own need for control, power, and wealth.

THE LAST YEAR OF MINISTRY

After a lengthy and much-needed rest, our rejuvenated group left Bethany and headed back to Galilee. As we traveled back along the same familiar routes, the numbers of followers began to grow, and soon we were inundated with people again.

The requests for healings and exorcizing increased dramatically, and it seemed that we were always busy and correspondingly fragmented. By now, news of Jesus had spread throughout all of Judea, Galilee, and Samaria, and word of his powers had been carried into many surrounding countries as well. He had become a celebrity, often for the wrong reasons. Jews continued to encourage him to lead a rebellion against the Romans, while the religious leaders grew in their hatred and intensified their attacks. We realized that now we were never free of the spies; they infiltrated the crowd at every moment.

Jesus became ever more assertive in his message, accusing the religious leaders of portraying a harsh, judgmental God who should be feared, rather than a loving, merciful God who should be approached in love and who wanted to draw all people to himself.

Jesus railed against the countless rules and regulations imposed by the Scribes and especially by the Pharisees, noting that the average Jew couldn't possibly know them all, let alone follow them. He exposed the fact that by promulgating the minutiae, the religious leaders were made to seem more holy, faithful, and learned than the everyday worshipers, which of course was their objective, and he castigated them for it.

Jesus continually called his listeners to instead meditate upon and then act upon the spirit of the Law, not just the letter of the Law. He fervently wanted to bring the people to the father; he posited a much gentler, loving God, and the religious leaders didn't know how to devalue his teaching so they responded with hateful animosity and an ardent desire to silence him. Jesus knew of course that the situation was headed toward a showdown, but his work was not yet done, so he traveled again to the friendlier atmosphere in Galilee.

One phenomenon worth mentioning was Jesus' intense love for children, and their love for him. Whenever he got the chance, he would get on the ground with them and talk to them about how much God cared for them by giving them beautiful birds and flowers and other wonderful manifestations of his love. Whereas he usually waited for those adults who needed healing to approach him, he nevertheless would enter the crowd and begin healing sick children without being asked, often healing ills of which neither the children nor their parents were aware. "These children are the delight of the Father," he would frequently tell us, and surely the children would remember Jesus long after he was gone because of his kindness to them. "Let the little children come to me," he would often say.

Jesus began taking what I considered to be a tougher stance when asked about eternal life; one time he suggested that sincere inquirers leave all of their wealth behind and follow him, and at another time he encouraged them to "take up your cross daily and follow me." His listeners understood him to mean the cross of crucifixion, and many turned away and did not come back. Indeed, many of his teachings were hard to accept.

More and more he taught in parables, and at times the crowds and even the apostles didn't grasp the point of the story. At such times, Jesus would take the apostles off alone and carefully teach them the truth that he was trying to convey via the parable.

In addition to the stubbornness of the religious leaders and the reluctance to change of the masses, Jesus also faced disappointments with the apostles. After over two years of listening to him almost daily, they nevertheless behaved in ways that obviously frustrated and disappointed him. For instance, the mother of James and John, no doubt acting at the request of her sons, asked Jesus if her two sons could sit on either side of him when he became king. Jesus responded that those positions were not his to give, but his Father's.

When the other ten apostles got wind of the scheme by James and John, they became indignant and were prepared to ostracize the two offenders. Jesus had to call everyone together, sort out the differences, and elaborate on a loftier perspective of the end times. Above all, he cautioned, they must be committed to providing loving service to one another and to the masses; loving service would be the hallmark of his followers.

Jesus had to address all manner of situations, all of which he did expertly. Questions arose about divorce, and about paying taxes, and about life after death. His exasperation with the religious leaders reached the boiling point, so he said to the crowds and his disciples: "Obey and follow everything they tell you to do; do not, however, imitate their actions, because they don't practice what they preach. Become servants for one another."

CHANGE IN STRATEGY

Jesus' fatigue became more and more apparent. People sought him out continually, and he couldn't easily meet all of the demands placed upon him. In order to have sufficient time to pray, he often had to hide not only from the masses, but also from his own apostles and disciples. Occasionally Shadow would wake me to join Jesus in the middle of the night, but at those times I just sat quietly, praying and providing him company. He seemed to like to have me present, not asking anything of him except to be with him.

Also, Jesus knew that he had antagonized the religious leaders to the boiling point, and sooner or later they would find a way to silence him. The answer, it seemed to him, was to empower the apostles to take over for him once he was silenced, but he realized that they were not yet deeply enough inculcated in his teachings to carry on without him.

Sometimes, just when he thought he had made significant progress, their humanity would take over, and petty bickering would break out among them. This exasperated Jesus to no end, because he thought that they should be beyond such actions, but they were not.

Consequently, Jesus made a decision to diminish the time he spent with the crowds and concentrate on more aggressively preparing the apostles for the work ahead. He led them to remote spots where he tried to instill in them the basic principles of his teaching, and he even resorted to teaching them in a boat on Lake Galilee to escape the pressing throng.

And so it was that one day, after refusing the Pharisee's request for a miracle proving that he had God's approval, he got into a boat and asked the apostles to take him to the east side of Lake Galilee. While in the boat, Jesus said "Take care and be on your guard against the yeast of the Pharisees and the yeast of Herod." The apostles started blaming one another, believing that Jesus had said this because they only had one loaf of bread.

Jesus's frustration showed as he reprimanded the twelve, making it clear that he was talking about the poisonous teaching of the non-believers, rather then the bread that they had forgotten to bring. "You saw me break five loaves and feed five thousand people," he said, "and then seven loaves to feed four thousand people. And still you do not understand what I am trying to teach you." Upon landing, he instructed Peter and Andrew to moor the boat and secure it more strongly than usual.

The band entered into Bethsaida. Jesus instructed the apostles to prepare for an extended absence away from family and friends. They were to take warm clothes and adequate provisions as if being away for a long time. While they were off buying food, I stayed with Jesus. A blind man approached and begged Jesus to touch him, believing that Jesus' touch alone would heal him. Jesus took the blind man by the hand and led him out of the village. I watched as Jesus spit on the man's eyes and then laid his hands on the man, asking "Can you see anything?" The man reported seeing people, but they looked like walking trees. Jesus again laid hands on him, and the man could see clearly. I promptly saw the metaphor; if only the apostles could see so clearly when touched by Jesus.

CAESAREA PHILIPPI

We journeyed up the east side of the Jordan River, passing through the last Jewish settlements and into pagan territory. Jesus ordered us to refrain from gleaning in the fields or picking fruit of any kind from the branches of trees. There were enough of us that we weren't overly concerned about robbers, but Jesus wanted to avoid antagonizing the town's people who watched us pass through. Eventually we reached the numerous pagan shrines built into the cliff high above the northern portion of the Jordan River.

There, accompanied by only the twelve apostles and myself, he bade us make a camp. When we were all settled, he gathered the apostles together and asked: "Who do people say that I am?" "Some say John the Baptist," they answered, "others say Elijah, while still others say Jeremiah or some other prophet." "What about you?" Jesus asked them, "who do you say that I am?" Peter promptly replied: "You are the Messiah, the son of the living God."

"Blest be you, Simon, son of John," Jesus said, "for this truth did not come to you from any human being, but it was given to you directly by my Father in heaven. And so I tell you, Peter, you are a rock, and on this rock foundation I will build my church, and not even death will be able to overcome it. I will give you the keys to the Kingdom of heaven; what you prohibit on earth will be prohibited in heaven, and what you permit on earth will be permitted in heaven." By his words Jesus indicated to the rest of us that Peter would become our leader, which surprised us because of Peter's impetuousness.

DIRE WARNING

Peter and Andrew had wisely brought small throw-nets, and they proceeded to catch a quantity of small fish while the rest of us started a fire and steamed the vegetables that had been bought in Bethsaida. With bread and some fruit, we enjoyed a fine meal.

Jesus went off to pray, and the rest of us, tired from the day's long walk, soon reclined around the dwindling fire and went to sleep. The next morning, we again enjoyed a simple yet filling meal, and then Jesus gathered us all together again.

"Soon I must go to Jerusalem and suffer much from the elders, the chief priests, and the teachers of the Law. I will be put to death, but three days later I will be raised to life." Peter quickly jumped up like a shot out of a cannon, grabbed Jesus by the arm, and led him away from the rest of us, apparently intending that we not hear what was said. However, the exchange between him and Jesus was so loud that we heard every word.

"God forbid that you suffer and die, Lord—that must never happen to you." We knew that Peter was acting out of his great love for Jesus, and out of his need to still have Jesus as his Master. But Jesus rebuked him harshly: "Get away from me, Satan! You are an obstacle in my way, because these thoughts of yours don't come from God, but from man." Peter was stung to the core by Jesus' words, and especially by being called "Satan," and he returned to the group crestfallen and very hurt. We all sat in silence.

For a long time, Jesus stayed alone in the grove of trees into which Peter had led him. He finally returned after regaining his composure, and squatting in front of Peter, he took Peter's face in is hands, and said lovingly: "It was not my intention to hurt your feelings, and I called you 'Satan' because that is the temptation that Satan presented to me at the very beginning and is always presenting to me now; to digress from my path and take an easier way. But that cannot be. I must walk the path my Father has set before me."

Then Jesus settled back onto a boulder and said to the apostles: "If anyone wants to come with me, he must forget himself, carry his cross, and follow me. For whoever wants to save his own life will lose it; but whoever loses his life for my sake will find it. Will a person gain anything if he wins the whole world but loses his life? Of course not! There is nothing he can give to regain his life. For the Son of Man is about to come in the glory of his Father with his angels, and then he will reward each one according to his deeds. I assure you there are some here who will not die until they have seen the Son of Man come as king." Jesus' words gave us a lot to think about, and we continued to sit silently.

We remained in the region for some time, with Jesus teaching us explicitly about the approaching Kingdom of God and our part in promoting it. Then our food began to run low, so we slowly made our way back to Bethsaida and our boat. We crossed back over into Galilee, and when we gathered on the shore, the men caught some more fish and we had a wonderful dinner under the stars. Then Jesus said: "The Son of Man is about to be handed over to men who will kill him; but three days later he will be raised to life."

ANTICIPATION

The ministry was never the same after Jesus' repeated warnings about his imminent suffering, death, and resurrection, especially since the apostles couldn't grasp the concept of being raised from the dead, even though they had witnessed Jesus raising others from the dead on a number of occasions. There was a pervasive sadness over the whole group, and we all wondered how we would function without Jesus. Some men wept openly.

Life returned to almost normal on the plains of Gennesaret, and the crowds again appeared seeking physical healings, demon expulsion, and other favors from Jesus. A pattern emerged; Jesus would teach the people in parables, and then retreat to secluded places and explain the meaning of the parables to the apostles. While there, he would pray for long periods of time, and although he hoped the apostles would follow his example, they instead usually sat in small groups and made idle chatter while waiting.

After a time, some sincere Pharisees approach Jesus and advised him to avoid going to Jerusalem, since Herod wanted to kill him. Jesus lamented: "Jerusalem, Jerusalem! You kill the prophets, you stone the messengers God has sent you! How many times I wanted to put my arms around all your people, just as a hen gathers her chicks under her wings, but you would not let me! And so your Temple will be abandoned. I assure you that you will not see me until the time comes when you say: 'God bless him who comes in the name of the Lord.' " Not long after we headed to Bethany, and then to Jerusalem and Jesus' death.

THE ROAD TO SALVATION

Like the others, I had heard Jesus proclaim, on a number of occasions, that he must go to Jerusalem, suffer at the hands of the chief priests and elders, die, and rise again on the third day. But it seemed that the apostles and disciples still couldn't believe that such was possible, and consequently they remained in a kind of dazed denial about the matter. I, however, took Jesus' words literally, and while I didn't completely understand why it was that his death was necessary, and also while I hoped with all of my heart that it didn't have to happen, I accepted that this would be our last pilgrimage to Jerusalem together.

We traveled slowly through Samaria. While Jews normally didn't stoop to acknowledge Samaritans, Jesus was loving to them all. The story of the Samaritan woman at the well had spread far and wide, and Jesus had performed many healings as he passed through their region at other times. Consequently we were welcomed as we journeyed along, and we all were given food and hospitality by these "close to the earth," sincere people.

Eventually we entered Judea, and while Jesus' demeanor did not seem to change, I had a sense of foreboding about the entire affair. I walked along behind those accompanying him, and as we progressed our numbers swelled significantly. Jesus strode steadily along, not seeming to pause and "take in" the views of the countryside as was his usual custom. Instead he gazed straight ahead, full of purpose, intent upon reaching the Holy City where the drama of salvation was destined to play out as good triumphed over evil.

BARTIMAEUS

We passed through Jericho, and Jesus continued to purposefully advance toward Jerusalem. On the outskirts of the town, a commotion was heard as someone tried to get Jesus' attention. Those accompanying Jesus tried to hush a blind beggar who was loudly crying out from his begging station at the side of the road. I hurried to the beggar's side, and he was a sight to behold indeed. His hair was uncut, tangled, and dirty, and his robe was soiled from the fresh animal droppings in which he had inadvertently sat. He was a most unsavory person, and everything about him seemed repulsive. By now, however, I had developed a great compassion for such unfortunates, so I was eager to help him.

Jesus sensed the disruption and saw me helping the beggar to his feet, and he motioned for both of us to approach him. The pitiful man threw off his soiled cloak and jumped up, and I led him along toward Jesus. He began weeping, as a lifetime of pain and shame came pouring forth out of him. "Cheer up," the standers-by told him, "for the master is summoning you." The man kept repeating "Jesus, Son of David, have mercy on me."

When we reached Jesus, Jesus opened his arms and embraced the now sobbing man. "What do you want me to do for you?" Jesus asked him. "Teacher," the blind man responded, "I want to see again." "Go," Jesus replied, "your faith has made you well." "I am Bartimaeus," the healed beggar said, "and your face is the first thing I've been able to see since my childhood. Your face shows me love, so now I will join your followers, and I will thank and praise your God forever. He is now my God too!"

BRIEFING

We reached the northeast side of the Mount of Olives at dusk, and Jesus bade us stop for the night. I was surprised that he didn't press on to Bethany to stay with Mary, Martha, and Lazerus, his close friends, but instead he seemed intent on reaching Jerusalem.

By now his followers had developed a routine for setting up camp for the night, and soon the cook-fires were sending wafting smoke into the air. After a supper of fish stew and bread, I retired to a private spot to rest and say my evening prayers. I must have fallen asleep there, because I was damp and stiff when Shadow nudged me awake during the middle of the night. I picked up my carry-bag and followed Shadow into the darkness.

We ascended the mountain, and soon I saw Jesus, silhouetted on the skyline against the bright moonlight. He sat quietly, but he seemed to be deep in thought rather than deep in prayer. We embraced and then I sat down near him. He got right to the point: "Now it all starts in earnest," he said. "I know that, and I wish I could stop it," I said, "but I heard you rebuke Peter for trying to dissuade you from your mission, so I'll not try to do that."

"Thank you," Jesus responded. "You must be strong for the apostles and disciples. They will go to pieces during this, and I'm counting on you to be a prayerful, confident and calm influence for them when they otherwise would panic." I silently nodded my head. To my surprise, that was the end of the conversation. We then both laid down and slept.

ENCOURAGEMENT

I awoke to see the morning tinges of pink appear in the east. To my utter and complete amazement, Jesus was still there with me. Every other time we had met like this, he was gone when I awoke in the morning; now, he continued to sleep as dawn broke around us.

I looked at him lovingly. There was so much to admire about him, and it seemed so wrong that he had to suffer and die when he had done nothing except heal people and encourage them to repent, to welcome the reestablished kingdom, and to love God.

It was mid-morning when Andrew and Phillip climbed the mountain and found us. Andrew handed each of us some fruit and bread, saying "Everyone's looking for you; what would you have us tell them?" "Let them rest a while longer," Jesus said. "In the meantime, go into the village directly ahead of us, where you will find a colt tethered to a gate. Untie him and bring him here, and if people ask what you are doing, tell them that the master has need of the animal and will return him promptly after we have used him."

The pair headed down the mountain, while Jesus and I continued to sit in silence, quietly watching the beautiful landscape while munching on our fruit. Jesus finally broke the silence once more: "Have courage, Elder David," he said, "for it will end well. You must believe that and share that belief with my followers. There will be very dark moments, but in the end good will prevail over evil. Be strong and believe in me."

APPROACHING DISASTER

Later in the morning we could see Andrew and Phillip returning from the village with the young donkey, and we arose and went half-way down the mountain to meet them. The large band of followers sensed that something big was about to happen, and they had broken camp and were awaiting Jesus on the path leading to Jerusalem. Everyone began walking together, and when the band crested the last ridge and saw Jerusalem across the Kidron Valley, Jesus stopped and gazed at the beautiful city bathed in sunlight.

At that point, he mounted the young donkey and began the steep, winding descent off of the mountain. Quickly the local inhabitants became aware of his passing, and children ran ahead to herald his coming to other residents along the way. Riding an animal was a symbol of power, and the local citizens soon joined in with the crowd, spreading their cloaks and putting branches along the roadway as if honoring a triumphant king. They shouted words of praise: "Praise God! God bless him who comes in the name of the Lord! God bless the coming kingdom of King David, our father! Praise be to God."

Unfortunately, their expectations and intentions were misdirected. As the crowd swelled, a sense of euphoria passed through it, as if the Messiah had appeared who would free them from Roman oppression and return Israel to power and prestige. An armed Roman centurion on a warhorse watched the crowd from a high vantage point, and the contrast between the powerful mounted soldier and the meek man on the colt was startling; Jesus would surely disappoint the masses.

Jesus rode calmly along, a look of serenity and acceptance on his face, broken only by smiles when he saw children waving at him and handing him flowers. By the time the procession crossed the Kidron Valley and approached the East Gate of the temple, the crowd had swelled to several thousand people, striking fear into the hearts of both the Romans who witnessed it and also the members of the Sanhedrin who feared that their power might be usurped by this very popular Rabbi. Surely such a show of force was threatening to the status quo, and both groups recognized that Jesus must be stopped.

The crowd had turned into an unruly, unsafe mob, and rational thinking could have easily been replaced with mob violence and insurrection if Jesus had at all encouraged it. The proceedings were visible from the Antonium, the Roman fortress situated next to and above the temple, and as Pontius Pilatus watched the scene he wondered whether his garrison had enough strength to quell an uprising of such magnitude if trouble occurred.

But somehow the mere pervasive presence of Jesus kept the crowd in check, and soon the entourage reached the temple itself, at which point many people left the area and returned to their homes. Jesus entered the temple and looked around, and the look that appeared on his face suggested that he didn't like what he saw. He called his followers into a side room where they prayed for a short while, and then at mid-afternoon he and the apostles left and headed for Bethany, where his friends warmly welcomed the entire group. I noted that Jesus still seemed disturbed by something he saw in the temple, but he was able to put it aside and thoroughly enjoy the hospitality of his close friends.

DECLARATION OF WAR

The next morning dawned overcast and gloomy. As I walked down to the outside courtyard where the apostles had slept, I was surprised to see Jesus already outside. Since Jesus usually seemed very relaxed and free after his morning prayer time, it was unusual to see him eager to be on his way. Beneath his composed exterior I sensed a tension; he seemed edgy, anxious, almost itching to get on with the day's events.

Shortly thereafter, Jesus rounded up the twelve apostles and headed back to Jerusalem. His stride was long and purposeful; there was no lingering today to enjoy the beauty of nature. On the way, he spotted a fig tree, and since he hadn't had breakfast, he went over to look for some figs to eat. Finding none, he declared the tree barren forever, which seemed harsh to us who heard him since it was not the time in which figs were in season.

Entering Jerusalem, Jesus headed directly for the temple. At the entrance, he found a heavy rope which had been left behind when the young bullock it had secured had been led into the temple for ritual sacrifice. He tied some large knots onto the end of the rope and headed inside the temple. The outer courtyard was bustling with commerce. All manner of sacrificial birds and animals were available for sale, and money changers offered to convert most foreign currencies into the coins prescribed for almsgiving. The courtyard seemed much more like a marketplace than a place of worship, and observing the din of greedy traders looking for a quick profit, Jesus became highly distressed.

The condemnation of the fig tree was nothing as compared to what happened next. I had seen Jesus angry with the hypocritical and hard-hearted Scribes and Pharisees, but now I witnessed physical fury as Jesus' anger boiled over and he rushed into the middle of the courtyard where he began turning over tables, spilling all of the coins as he went. He opened bird cages and released the birds, and swinging his rope, he drove the larger sacrificial animals outside onto the street. Seeing his controlled rage, no one dared try to stop him, and he did not rest until the entire commercial enterprise was undone.

The scene looked like a massive storm had swept through the courtyard. There were coins scattered everywhere. Moneychangers on their hands and knees scurried to recover their own money while also greedily trying to steal the money of their competitors. They commenced to push and shove one another, fights broke out, and pandemonium reigned. Jesus intervened and would not let anyone carry anything through the temple courtyard.

Jesus eventually regained his composure and entered into the inner courtyard, where many devout Jews were praying. The moneychangers and merchants banded together and followed him there, and began demanding an explanation for his unsettling actions.

He replied: "It is written in the Scriptures that God said 'My Temple will be called a house of prayer for the people of the nations.' But you have turned it into a hideout for thieves!" The whole crowd stood stunned in light of his actions and especially his teaching, and all were amazed at the authority he demonstrated. At that point, Jesus led the faithful in prayers of atonement and then he and the apostles departed for Bethany.

Word of the event quickly reached the chief priests and teachers of the law, and they were infuriated because they perceived themselves as being in control of the temple, and more so because the money-changing and animal-selling operations were huge sources of income with which they filled the temple coffers while also filling their personal purses.

A meeting of the most influential religious leaders was convened, and it was quickly recognized that this Rabbi was garnering an increasing number of faithful followers while also challenging the traditional teachings and functioning of the Jewish religion. They were afraid of him and his power, and they recognized that his actions were tantamount to a challenge to their authority. Up until now, he had been a troublesome nuisance who called them names and challenged their orthodoxy, but now he had invaded their home turf and had thrown down the gauntlet as to how the temple should be operated.

Clearly the religious leaders' emphasis on the money-making aspect of temple commerce had been exposed as less than the lofty purpose for which the temple had been intended, and the people were beginning to see how hypocritical the leaders actually were. Jesus' teachings about their ways was problematic enough for them when he was in Galilee, but now his confrontation of them in Judea was more than they could tolerate.

During their meeting, they spent much time formulating challenging questions with which to confront him, while also resolving to try to find a way to have him killed. His murder would have to be well planned so as not to arouse the people or the Romans.

PONDERING

That evening I left the busy-ness of the house in Bethany and climbed up onto the mountain to be alone. I was deeply disturbed. While I would have hoped that there could have been some dialogue and then some ensuing agreement between Jesus and the religious leaders, I understood that such an agreement would have involved extensive compromise on the parts of both parties, and such compromise was anathema to both.

While the apostles were stunned by what had happened in the temple, they were loath to talk about it and seemed to want to push it into the backs of their memories, something like a bad dream from the distant past. But I saw the event for what it was: a final challenge from Jesus to the religious leaders to restore the sacredness of the temple, which in turn would symbolize their willingness to restore the sacredness of the religion.

Consequently, I saw that what Jesus had warned us about would now happen quite quickly; Jesus had hastened his own suffering and death by confronting them in their own seat of power and insisting that God their Father was not pleased with their banal governing. I silently wept for a good part of the night, knowing that this fine, virtuous, loving man would have to suffer and die for his principles, leaving the rest of us leaderless. When I returned to the patio where the apostles had slept, Jesus approached me and looked at me. He must have seen my red eyes from weeping and lack of sleep because in an extremely poignant gesture he squeezed my hand, and said: "I'm sorry that you have to suffer too."

RETURN TO THE TEMPLE

As Jesus again headed for Jerusalem, the apostles observed that the fig tree that Jesus had cursed had already died. What surprised them was that in a day's time, it had withered all the way down to its roots. Jesus used the discovery to teach the apostles about the power of prayer and to encourage them to ask the Father for what they needed.

As we approached the temple, the expected happened and we were accosted by a sizable group of religious leaders. Their question had been carefully derived and their challenge was immediate: "What right do you have to do these things?" they asked, "Who gave you such a right?" One thing I had noticed about Jesus over and over again was that he was an excellent strategist and could think quickly on his feet. Never in three years had they bested him in face-to-face argumentation, and this time would be no exception. Jesus responded with a question, as he often did, telling the leaders that if they answered his question, he would then answer theirs. He queried them about John's right to baptize, and they realized they were trapped; any answer they gave would indict them. Their answer, therefore, was a lame "We don't know," after which they slunk away.

By now, a large crowd had assembled to witness the exchange, and after the religious leaders left, Jesus used the opportunity to teach the people using a number of parables.

Later, some bitter Jewish leaders returned with some temple guards in an attempt to arrest Jesus, but seeing the size of the crowd he had attracted, they left him alone and departed.

JESUS' FINAL APPEARANCE IN THE TEMPLE

The third day was a repeat of the previous two days. We returned to the temple where Jesus prayed and then began to teach the crowds. Some Pharisees and members of Herod's party were the first snipers to appear in the crowd, trying to trap Jesus with questions about paying taxes. Jesus handled their trick question with candor and brilliance, and they went away amazed at the wisdom and clear thinking he exuded.

His teaching was again interrupted a while later by the Sadducees, another religious group that did not believe in life after death. They too had devised a trick question to trap Jesus, but he again answered it in a way that confounded them instead of himself. He didn't miss the opportunity to attack their hard-headedness: "How wrong you are! And do you know why? It is because you don't know the Scriptures or God's power—you are completely wrong indeed!" They too realized they were defeated and disappeared.

Next a teacher of the Law questioned Jesus, but he was a sincere man who had heard Jesus' response to the Sadducees and who was seeking the deeper truths he hoped Jesus could provide. Jesus patiently entered into a dialogue with the teacher because he saw the man's sincerity. He answered the man's question about the greatest commandment, and at the end of the respectful exchange Jesus pronounced the teacher "not far from the Kingdom of God." After that, nobody dared to ask Jesus any more questions.

After a long day of parrying the religious leaders' thrusts, a frustrated Jesus said: "Watch out for the teachers of the Law who like to walk around in their long robes and be greeted with respect in the marketplace, who choose the reserved seats in the synagogues and the best places at feasts. They take advantage of widows and rob them of their homes, and then make a show of saying long prayers. Their punishment will be all the worse!"

"There is an example of what I mean," he continued. "While the rich people make a show of depositing their excess money in the Temple treasury box, that small frail widow over there quietly dropped in two copper coins, which is all of the money she has in this world. Poor as she is, she put in all she had—she gave all that she had to live on. Who is more worthy of the Kingdom of God in God's eyes?" he concluded, "who but the widow!"

Jesus continued to teach until mid-afternoon, at which point he gathered the apostles in preparation for leaving. As they passed through the temple portal, one follower was heard to exclaim "Look Teacher! What wonderful stones and buildings." Jesus responded: "You see these great buildings? Not a single stone will be left in its place; every one of them will be thrown down." Some of his listeners doubted the accuracy of his statement.

The small band returned to the home of Mary, Martha and Lazarus, where we were again treated to warm hospitality and a great dinner. I sensed that Jesus was preoccupied with his thoughts, but he did his best to be present to everyone. After supper, the apostles and I retired to the outside patio while Jesus remained inside to converse with his friends.

RESPITE

The next morning, Jesus seemed to linger over breakfast with his friends. Eventually, however, he bade them good-by and we left their spacious domicile. Little did they know what lie ahead for him and for all of us, although knowing him well, they must have sensed his tension and preoccupation, since it seemed that he was unable to fully relax.

At a fork in the path, Jesus surprised us by heading up the mountain instead of toward Jerusalem. We ascended the Mount of Olives until we reached the spot where Jesus and I had had our first meetings months before. We sat on the boulders, looking across at the Temple, so white and beautiful in the bright sunshine. It was like a day of rest and relaxation, sitting in the sun, praying privately, and conversing with one another.

Four of the apostles approached Jesus in private and asked for a further explanation of his prediction that not a single stone of the Temple would be left in place. Instead of telling just the four, Jesus gathered us all together and spent much of the day prophesizing about the destruction of the Jewish state, and further, about the end of the world and the second coming of the "Son of Man." At the time, none of us fully grasped what he was saying.

It was an unusual day. Jesus seemed somber, and he spent much time warning us about the chaos and destruction to come. He used the withered fig tree as an example of how quickly things (and people) could be struck and killed. He warned us we would not know the time when this would occur so we should stay alert. We did not question him further.

Finally, Jesus made the connection to his own life by telling us directly and explicitly that in two days' time he would be handed over to suffer, be crucified and die. I watched the apostles' faces, and it seemed that they found it impossible to comprehend such a thing.

Toward evening, we headed down the mountain toward Bethany, but instead of going to the home of Mary, Martha and Lazarus, Jesus led us to the house of Simon, a man whom Jesus had cured of leprosy. There, while Jesus reclined at dinner, a woman entered the room, and falling at his feet, she broke open a jar of very expensive perfume and anointed his feet with it, wiping the excess off with her hair.

While many of the apostles and other guests were privately appalled at the apparent waste of a very valuable commodity, Judas was openly critical and harshly condemned her action. Jesus defended her, noting that she was preparing him in advance for his burial, and promising that she would forevermore be remembered for her kindness and love.

While Jesus did not focus his admonition directly at Judas, Judas was nevertheless stung by Jesus' words. Judas excused himself, mentioning that he had things to attend to in Jerusalem. This wasn't unusual, since Judas at times left the rest of us to be about his own affairs, and we recognized that he wasn't fully committed to being part of our group.

Although it was evening, Judas traversed the lengthy path into Jerusalem. We learned later that the chief priests and elders were already meeting and making plans to arrest Jesus. Judas' arrival at their meeting and offer to betray Jesus came at an opportune time.

BEGINNING OF THE SOJOURN

The next morning, Jesus, the apostles, and myself left Simon's home and headed toward Jerusalem. Near the Mount of Olives, Jesus sent the apostles ahead to the city to prepare the Passover meal, instructing them as to whom to approach and what to say regarding the place we would meet. He beckoned me to join him on the climb to our usual prayer spot. We both knew what was about to transpire; we spent the day in silence and prayer.

At mid-afternoon, Jesus and I descended the mountain and crossed the Kidron Valley, entering Jerusalem through the East Gate and making our way to the private, upper room Jesus had specified. I was not offended that there was not a place prepared for me at the table. I accepted the fact that I was somewhat of an anomaly, and I was comfortable taking a seat on a windowsill from whence I could view the beautiful city below.

When everyone had reclined at table, Jesus surprised us by rising, removing his outer cloak, and wrapping a towel around his waist. Deferential as always, Jesus came to me first, and before I could protest, he began washing my feet, which was a humbling experience for me indeed. He then moved to the table and began washing the feet of the twelve apostles. Peter created a stir by at first refusing to allow Jesus to wash his feet, but after an exchange which I could not hear, Peter finally allowed the washing to occur.

Jesus then put his outer garment back on and again reclined at table, and the meal began. The atmosphere was somber and tense, but Jesus calmly led us through the Passover rite.

During the meal, just as he handed Judas Iscariot a piece of bread dipped in a mixture of olive oil and bitter herbs, Jesus announced loudly: "I tell you, one of you will betray me." The apostles became very upset at this news, and began to ask him, one after the other, "Surely, Lord, you don't mean me?" Judas remained silent until all of the others had asked, and he then said: "Surely, Teacher, you don't mean me?" Jesus looked at him with compassion and pity, looked at him so as to see his very soul, and sadly replied: "It is as you say." With that, Judas abruptly rose from the table and hurried from the room.

There was stunned silence in the room for a lengthy period of time. Then Jesus looked back at me and gestured that I should come forward and take Judas' place at the table. We continued the meal, although the atmosphere was now charged with growing dread. Taking a piece of bread, Jesus broke the silence by giving a prayer of thanks to God, broke it into twelve pieces, and passing a piece to each of us, he said: "Take and eat, for this is my body." Then, taking a cup of wine, he gave thanks to God and passed the cup to each of us, saying: "Drink, all of you, for this is my blood which seals God's covenant, my blood poured out for many for the forgiveness of sins. I tell you, I will never again drink this wine until the day I drink the new wine with you in my Father's kingdom."

After a pause, Jesus said: "I tell you, this very night all of you will run away and leave me." The apostles began to protest, and Peter loudly debated Jesus' assertion, saying that he would never leave Jesus, even if the rest did. Jesus quietly said to him: "I tell you that before the rooster crows you will deny me three times." "Never," Peter said, "Never!"

DEATH MARCH

We left the upper room, and Jesus led us out of the city and to a beautiful grove of olive trees at the base of the Mount of Olives. He left most of us on the edge of the grove, and took Peter, James and John with him deeper into the garden. The remaining nine of us made a bit of small talk, but there was a graveness to all of our demeanors, and after a short while each of us sat with our own thoughts, and many of us eventually fell asleep.

After a lengthy time, Jesus roused us and we started walking out of the garden. I looked at his face and I could already see the anguish and strain. He was pale and his features were drawn. He looked gaunt and very tired. I sensed his dread about what was coming.

Looking toward the city, I saw the night lit up with a large number of torches, and Jesus bravely walked toward the approaching figures. It was a motley group of temple guards and other onlookers—a bunch of thugs spoiling for trouble. Jesus confronted them and they all backed away. Finally Judas stepped forward and kissed Jesus, having instructed the guards that that would be the sign by which they'd know which man to arrest.

Chaos broke out. As they seized Jesus and began to fasten a rope around his wrists, Peter drew a sword and swung at the head of a servant of the high priest, cutting off his ear. Jesus ordered Peter to put the sword away, but the sword had brought the attention of the mob onto the apostles, and the armed guards began approaching Jesus' followers.

They reached for the young John, but he slipped out of his clothes and ran away naked. "Leave them all alone," Jesus said, "for it is I that you came to arrest. Let the rest go free." The guards realized that they had been sent to arrest Jesus only, so they again turned their attention to him and began leading him back toward the city, shoving and hitting him as they went. The apostles all fled for their lives, while I followed along behind the crowd. Seeing me, one of the guards with a club left the group and dropped back to accost me, but Shadow suddenly manifested himself and the guard retreated quickly. Jesus looked back, and seeing me, quietly instructed me to leave and go to where the Sanhedrin was meeting. I was loathe to leave Jesus, not wanting to abandon him as had the rest, but he again firmly instructed me to go to the Sanhedrin meeting.

I feared having to walk past the entire mob to follow the path into the city, but Shadow headed off in a different direction through the dark night and I followed closely behind. He again chose a small, almost indistinguishable game trail that was a short-cut. It was gently sloped and stone free, and I soon found myself back on the main path but significantly ahead of the torch-bearing crowd.

Shadow led me to a different spot than I had been used to, and I found myself at the house of the High Priest, Caiaphas, where the most powerful members of the Sanhedrin were meeting. Although I had been absent for a long time, I was still an appointed Elder and no one questioned my presence as I took a seat. A few of my former acquaintances nodded a tepid greeting. I immediately felt uncomfortable because they were rehearsing how the imminent trial of Jesus would be held, and they knew I was his loyal follower.

THE TRIAL

What they called a trial was instead a travesty. Jesus was brought in like a common criminal, and he had already been mistreated and was bleeding from a number of blows. Supposed witnesses were brought forward to testify with carefully conceived evidence, but their testimonies didn't corroborate with one another and I knew all of it was false.

Caiaphas became increasingly frustrated and angry. Jesus was a threat to his personal power, prestige and wealth, and the Sanhedrin must find a way to condemn him to death. Jesus answered none of the charges, which infuriated the priests and elders further, and one guard punched Jesus in the face in retaliation for Jesus' apparent insolence in not trying to defend himself. Caiaphas finally said: "In the name of the living God I now put you under oath: tell us if you are the Messiah, the Son of God."

"It is as you say," Jesus replied. "But I tell you this," Jesus continued, "from this time on you will see the Son of Man sitting at the right hand of the Almighty and coming on the clouds of heaven." Caiaphas was beside himself with impatience and fury, and in a dramatic gesture, he tore his clothes and instructed the assembly that Jesus must die.

I rose from my seat and stormed to the front of the assembly, full of indignant rage. "This is an outrage of justice," I said, and as the howls of derision started, I spoke even louder. "This man has done nothing except to love us and heal us and encourage us to love God and fulfill our obligations to one another in a compassionate manner."

A few others of the assembly quietly urged caution in the matter, noting that Jesus was very popular with the masses and that the leaders really didn't have a case against him. Caiaphas shouted each one down in turn while also inciting his allies to drown out the few who were reluctant to put Jesus to death. "They are right," I shouted at Caiaphas.

Caiaphas looked down at me with a look of hatred, and said: "You are one of his followers, and you have chosen his false religion instead of the faith of our fathers Abraham and Isaac and Jacob. I command you, sit down and be silent." "I will not," I replied, "until you realize you are condemning an innocent man who has done no wrong."

"You no longer are welcome in this assembly," Caiaphas screamed. "Remove him," he said to a guard standing near him. As the guard dragged me toward the door, I shouted loudly over my shoulder: "You are a mob of criminals and a disgrace to our religion, and surely not worthy heirs of our fathers. You will be held accountable for this murder, and may God treat you as you are treating Jesus."

Outside, I spotted Peter and John in the courtyard and joined them near a warming fire. "It does not go well in there," I told them; "they are planning on killing Jesus." The three of us knew that we were among a hostile crowd, and we were uncomfortable and afraid. When various individuals noted Peter's affiliation to Jesus, John and I heard him deny such a relationship three times. When the cock crowed, Peter realized what he had done, and knowing that he had disgraced himself in front of us, he rushed away into the night.

PONTIUS PILATUS

Word spread quickly through the courtyard that Jesus had been condemned to death. Out of the darkness Judas appeared, and bursting into the meeting room, he tried to undo the deal he had made by giving back the thirty pieces of silver he had received for his betrayal. "I have sinned by betraying an innocent man to death," he wailed. "What do we care about that?", the leaders responded, "that is your business." The eyes of Judas and Jesus met in a poignant exchange, and then Judas ran from the room; we learned later he had thrown the silver pieces onto the temple floor and went out and hanged himself.

It was the middle of the night when the leaders emerged from Caiaphas' house. Orders were given to the guards and servants to round up as many sympathizers to the leaders' position as possible, and to have them join the entourage headed for the Antonium. Once a large crowd had been gathered, the leaders incited them with false charges about Jesus.

The crowd became a frenzied mob, at which point Jesus was led out and everyone headed for the Roman fortress. Once there, the leaders asked the Roman soldiers to rouse Pilatus from his sleep, since they had a pressing matter to discuss with him which could not wait until morning. They did this because they wanted the death sentence levied before any of Jesus' followers were aware of it and before any opposition to the leaders could develop. Pilatus was not pleased with the disruption to his sleep. Jerusalem was full of pilgrims celebrating the Passover, and a mass riot might be more than his garrison could handle.

Pilatus was an astute strategist and politician, and he immediately began looking for a way by which he could extricate himself from this dangerous situation. At first he thought the whole matter to be a monstrous imposition on his time and attention. The man in front of him was bloodied and his clothing soiled, and he seemed an everyday kind of person who surely could not be a threat to the Jewish leaders. But as Pilatus looked more closely at Jesus, he sensed an inner calm, strength and courage that was unusual to behold. As he began questioning Jesus, his conviction deepened that here was an unusual man, a man of God who had done nothing but rub the leaders the wrong way.

Pilatus was cunning and he had spies everywhere; if Jesus had preached treason or encouraged the nonpayment of taxes to the Romans, he would have heard about it by now. The leaders continued to press their case, saying that Jesus had positioned himself as king of the Jews, while the leaders contended that they had no king but Caesar. Pilatus inwardly scoffed at this assertion, and recognized their crafty maneuvers for what they were. But he was curious about the "king" issue, so as part of his questioning he asked Jesus: "Are you the king of the Jews?" Jesus replied "It is as you say, but my kingdom is not of this world. If it was, my followers would be fighting for me, but it is not of this world. Just as your authority comes from Caesar, my authority comes from elsewhere."

Pilatus became increasingly impressed with Jesus, and when he learned that he was a Galilean, Pilatus saw his way out of the situation. Since Herod was Tetrarch of Galilee, he would let Herod make the ruling, especially since Herod was in Jerusalem at the time.

HEROD

The leaders had mixed emotions about being referred onward to Herod. They knew that they might have more leverage with him since he was a Jew, but they also knew that he was temperamental and impetuous and not as likely to be persuaded by sound arguments.

The mob started through the city, and I followed at a distance. By now I had been two days with little sleep, and fatigue was starting to set in; nevertheless, I pressed onward.

Herod was pleased to have the opportunity to meet Jesus because he had heard a great deal about him and had been eager to meet him for a long time. Also, he wished to have a bit of sport at Jesus' expense, while also hoping that Jesus might perform some miracles for him. The chief priests and the teachers of the Law stepped forward and made many accusations about Jesus, but Herod correctly discerned their motives and discounted their testimony. Instead, he spent a significant amount of time questioning Jesus, but Jesus knew that Herod had had John the Baptist killed and did not think highly of his cousin's murderer, and consequently, Jesus did not answer any of Herod's questions.

Seeing Jesus' unwillingness to cooperate, Herod gave him over to his soldiers, who made fun of him and treated him with contempt. They finally put a fine purple robe on him and sent him back to Pilatus. We all retraced our steps to the Antonium. Pilatus saw humor in Herod's move, and the two changed from enemies to friends that day because of it.

THE VERDICT

By now, the crowd had grown into an unruly mob, spurred on by the priming of the chief priests and other religious leaders. Pilatus was not pleased that Jesus' fate was now back in his hands, since he faced a conundrum in that he wished to release Jesus but feared an outbreak of violence if he did so. He called the religious leaders aside and told them that neither he nor Herod had found Jesus guilty of any of the crimes of which they had accused him, so Pilatus' intention was to have Jesus whipped and then set free.

While Jesus was taken inside the Antonium to be scourged, the religious leaders began fomenting the crowd to ask for the release of Barabbas, an insurrectionist and murderer. Pilatus continued to try to reason with the crowd, saying that the religious leaders had not made a satisfactory case against Jesus, and consequently Pilatus intended to release him.

The decision was temporarily suspended until the scourging of Jesus was completed. The soldiers had had great sport with Jesus, beating him repeatedly while mocking him as well. All their hatred for the despicable Jews and for their assignment in this lonely outpost so far from their homes in Rome was transmitted via the whip onto Jesus' back and sides. Jesus remained silent during the whipping, and the soldiers intensified the scourging in an attempt to "break him," but he did not utter a sound. When the soldiers brought him back, again clothed in the purple robe and with a crown of thorns hammered into his scalp, he was very weak, covered with blood, and beaten nearly senseless.

And yet, Jesus stood with a dignified stance and a calm demeanor. Pilatus again questioned Jesus in an attempt to find a way to free him. The religious leaders employed a new strategy and told Pilatus that if he freed Jesus, he was no friend of Caesar's.

The tactic worked, since Pilatus feared Caesar's wrath and knew that the Jews had pipelines to Rome. In the middle of the discussion, Pilatus' wife sent a dire warning to him advising him not to condemn Jesus to death, further complicating his decision.

Pilatus went back out to the crowd and showed them Jesus. "Here is your king," he told the throng, "do you want me to crucify your king?" The religious leaders quickly and loudly shouted back: "The only king we have is the Emperor." Pilatus then ordered a basin of water be brought to him in which he washed his hands, symbolically absolving himself of any further involvement in the matter. He then handed Jesus over to the mob.

I was revolted by what they had done to Jesus, and my stomach was sick over the cruel punishment they had already inflicted. When Pilatus then said to the Jews, "Take him yourselves and crucify him," something inside me snapped and I pushed forward through the crowd, hurrying up the steps onto the raised platform to confront Pilatus directly. "You mustn't do this," I pleaded, "this man has done nothing but love us and heal us and encourage us to be good people. These men seek his death because they are threatened by his goodness." As I touched Pilatus' arm while further pleading Jesus' case, my efforts were interrupted by a flash of excruciating pain in my head, and then there was darkness.

CLAVICUS

Cold water being poured on my head roused me from unconsciousness. I look up to see a young soldier holding the basin in which Pilatus had washed his hands as his disclaimer of any involvement in the death of Jesus. How ironic, I thought, that the waters of shameful guilt were used to return me to awareness. "What happened to me?" I asked the legionnaire. "You got too close to Pilatus, and I...er, I mean a soldier, hit you with the butt of his spear. You're lucky he didn't run you through with the sharp spear-point. Now get up and get out of here, old man, before we scourge you also," he said scornfully.

I struggled to raise myself up on one elbow. The Antonium was empty except for the two of us. "Where have they taken him?" I asked. "If you mean the imposter who thinks that he's king, they've taken him off to be crucified," he replied. "No," I screamed, "we must go and stop them." "I'm afraid it's a little too late for that," the soldier said, "they've been gone for quite some time. I need to go there as soon as I get you out of here."

I tried to rise but collapsed back onto the ground. I saw that I was covered with blood, and that there was more of my blood in a pool on the pavement. My head hurt unmercifully. Again I tried to rise off the ground but could not. The soldier finally grabbed me and angrily pulled me to my feet. I tried to do his bidding, but I was too weak to function. Finally I began to stagger forward, but I was woozy and fell heavily against him. "Lean on me," he said roughly, "and we'll go there together."

THE SORROWFUL WAY

"What is your name?", I asked him. "Clavicus," he said. "I have one more year in this hell-hole," he continued, "and then I can go home. I am counting the days." We proceeded slowly, with me leaning heavily on the strong young man. I sensed that beneath his gruff exterior, he was gentle and caring, but he could not let it show.

As we proceeded out of the Antonium, we reached the busy marketplace sector of the city, and the streets were crowded with people, busily preparing for the Sabbath. Our progress slowed to a near halt until Shadow manifested himself. Clavicus jumped back and reached for his sword. "Watch out for the wolf," he said, obviously startled. "He will not hurt you," I reassured him. "Where did he come from?", Clavicus asked, obviously still afraid of Shadow. "He is my guardian," I replied; "he will not hurt you."

"If he is your guardian, why didn't he protect you when I…er, I mean the soldier hit you?" he asked. "I don't know," I said, "but I do know that there was a good reason." "Some guardian," Clavicus scoffed, "to let you get hurt when he could have intervened."

With Shadow walking ahead of us the crowds quickly parted and we proceeded on our way. "Why are you so loyal to this Jesus, this rabble-rouser?", Clavicus asked. I paused and then decided to bare my soul. "This man you call a rabble-rouser is the finest man I've ever met. Those of us who have gotten close to him believe that he is the Messiah whom the Jews have long awaited. He is a man of love, peace and integrity. He is God!"

Clavicus sneered derisively. "We have lots of gods in Rome," he said, "and they don't seem to be of much use for anything." "We Jews believe in one true God," I continued, "and we have been in relationship with that God since the beginning of time. When we became unfaithful and fell away, some of our holy men prophesized that our God would come to earth to call us back to deep friendship with Him. I believe with all of my heart that this Jesus whom you are crucifying is God made man so that we might be saved."

"If the Jews have waited so long for this god-man to arrive, then why do they want him killed?" Clavicus asked, obviously perplexed. "Our religious leaders are horribly corrupt, and this Jesus has exposed their greed and their lack of a deep relationship with God. He has announced a kingdom of love and mercy, and he has encouraged the people to repent of their sins and to believe in the good news that he brings. He helped the people see how hypocritical, authoritarian and misguided the leaders are, and the leaders resent it."

"Ultimately, the leaders realized that they were losing control of the people and of the people's purses, and it was too much for them to tolerate. They were deaf to his pleas that they change their hearts, and instead became more and more stubborn in their ways."

"So now his attempts to bring the Jewish people back to God are thwarted by his death," Clavicus asserted. "Now it's all over, isn't it?" "No," I said, looking directly at him, "for he promised that he would come back from the dead on the third day and continue his work among us." Clavicus snorted indignantly. "Back from the dead?" he said, "believe me, when we Romans crucify a man, he is dead forever. Back from the dead, indeed!"

DEATH WATCH

As Clavicus literally dragged me up the hill, my eyes beheld three crosses silhouetted on the dark skyline, each supporting the body of a man. As we drew closer, the horror of the scene began to engulf me, and I could hardly continue toward the grisly sight. A band of religious leaders and curiosity-seekers stood back at quite a distance, and directly under the middle cross I saw the apostle John along with the mother of Jesus and a few other women including Myriam, whom I had thought of often in the years since I had seen her.

I pointed to a spot mid-way between the crowd and the cross, and Clavicus led me too it. He looked around and found a small dead tree limb that I could use as a staff to support myself. "Don't move from this spot and don't try anything heroic," he said, "or I will have to deal with you harshly, and I'd prefer to not have to do that." He walked away.

I looked up at Jesus, and he met my gaze. I was sick to the core with what I saw. Every inch of his body was covered with wounds and blood. The thorns were still imbedded in his scalp, and he had been nailed to the cross instead of being tied to it. The Romans had spared no effort to make his death as painful as possible, and he writhed in agony as he suffered. I thought of Zechariah introducing me to the prophecies of Isaiah so many years ago, and the words of Simeon and Anna at Jesus' presentation. Surely this man on the cross was the suffering Messiah of whom they all spoke.

I was numb with grief, and I could do nothing but stand there in silence, supported by my staff, Shadow at my side.

The two thieves, one on either side of Jesus, mocked Jesus and tormented him cruelly for a while; then one of the thieves came to his senses and reprimanded the other, noting that they deserved their punishment but that Jesus did not. Turning to Jesus, he asked for pardon and redemption, and Jesus promised him he would be in paradise that very day.

Clavicus came back to my side, carrying a skin full of water. "Here, old man," he said, "you're probably thirsty." I gulped the water quickly, and it occurred to me that I was probably dehydrated from all of the blood I had lost. "He promised that thief a place in paradise," Clavicus said. "What does that mean?" "Some of us Jews believe in life after death, and we further believe that those of us who lead an upright life will spend eternity in a wonderful place, devoid of all the pains and hardships of this world."

"Well how can he promise a low-life criminal eternal life in such a place?" Clavicus persisted. "We believe that people can repent and return to God at any time, even in the last moments of their lives." "That belief makes life here on earth more bearable, doesn't it?" Clavicus retorted, and then left my side to return to the group of other soldiers.

I continued to gaze at the face of Jesus, and I began to pray that he would die quickly so as to not have to suffer any longer. A short while later, Clavicus returned again. "This man is unlike any other we've ever crucified," he said; "he seems to have calmness and dignity in the midst of truly unbearable pain. He asked his father, whoever that is, to forgive all of us who crucified him, saying that we don't know what we're doing."

"His father is the one true God of Israel," I noted. "Then who is this Jesus?", Clavicus asked. "Jesus is the son of the Father. They are both aspects of the same one true God." "How can that be?" Clavicus queried. "They are two manifestations of the same reality," I said, "like Shadow, my guardian, is sometimes visible and sometimes not, and yet he is one and the same entity." "This is hard to swallow," Clavicus said, and walked away.

I was left alone with my thoughts. I pondered how mankind could be so inhumanly cruel. The visage on the cross was hideous, gruesome, pitiful, and yet the religious leaders and soldiers continued to taunt Jesus, even in his final minutes. How could God let his son suffer like this, and why was it even necessary, I wondered. And further, what kind of a supposedly good God, a God of love and mercy, could let this happen in the first place?

Clavicus returned. "You say he will come back to life in three days. I say that that is impossible, especially when we get done with him." "All things are possible with God," I noted. "I have seen him raise several people from the dead," I said. "Magic," Clavicus responded, "pure trickery." "One of Jesus' friends had been dead for four days," I said, "and there was a strong stench already emanating from his tomb. Jesus raised him from the dead, and a large number of people witnessed it, including several religious leaders." "Then why don't they believe in him?" Clavicus asked sarcastically. "Because they are hard-hearted," I replied, "and if they accepted him and his teaching, they would have to repent and turn away from their greedy, power-hungry ways and become servants of the people as they are called to be." Clavicus shrugged his shoulders and walked away.

It didn't seem possible that Jesus' suffering could become worse, but it did. He had more and more difficulty pushing himself upright using the nails in his feet as support, and consequently each and every breath became more and more of a struggle for him. He cried out in thirst, and he cried out in pain over the apparent abandonment by his father.

Clavicus returned to my side yet another time. "It was I who hit you with the spear-butt," he said. "I know," I said, "I already surmised that, and I have forgiven you." "How could you forgive me for inflicting such a grave injury?" he asked; "I might have killed you!" "Jesus teaches us to love our enemies and forgive those who persecute us. I thought about it, and I realize that you were just doing your duty by protecting Pilatus."

Clavicus was taken aback. "I'm sorry I hit you so hard, old man" he said, "I could have just grabbed you and pulled you away. I have a lot of anger about being assigned here to this wretched place, and I took it out on you." "I understand," I said, "and I forgive you."

"I want you to have this," he said, putting something in my carry-bag, "as kind of a peace offering from me." "You don't need to do that, Clavicus" I said; "there's already peace between us. I appreciate your helping me get here, and the water too." "I want you to have it," he responded; "it's my share of the 'spoils' but it means nothing to me and I will just gamble it away, while I know it will mean a great deal to you." I looked in my carry-bag and saw Jesus' prayer shawl there, somehow spotlessly white, totally devoid of soiling or blood. "Think of me when you look at it he said," his voice breaking; "I have come to admire your faith and your loyalty to Jesus. I won't soon forget this day."

"I've figured out why Shadow didn't stop you from hitting me," I said. "If he had intervened, I wouldn't have met you and I wouldn't have had the opportunity to witness to you about Jesus." Clavicus nodded and slowly walked away.

I was numb with grief and sorrow, and I simply stood there looking at my suffering God. At last Jesus cried out "It is finished," and then "Father! Into your hands I commend my spirit," and mercifully he bowed his head and died. Just then a massive earthquake shook the earth and the sky turned darker than the dark of night. All of the soldiers were moved to their core, and their leader looked up at Jesus and said "He really was the Son of God."

Since it was the eve of the Sabbath, the religious leaders asked Pilatus if the legs of those crucified could be broken so as to ensure that they died from asphyxiation before sunset. Pilatus agreed and sent word to the soldiers to break the prisoners legs. They broke the legs of the two thieves, but seeing that Jesus was dead, they did not break his legs. Clavicus, wanting even more assurance that he was dead, pierced Jesus' heart with his sharp spear. Walking over to me, the blood and lymph still dripping from his spear, he quietly said "If he rises on the third day after what I have just done, I too will believe."

The soldiers, eager to return to their garrison and put the day's grisly work behind them, sprang into action. They took the two thieves down off their crosses first, and since no one was there to claim the bodies, they dragged them to a nearby pit that served as a rubbish heap for the populace and also an open burial site for the riff-raff of the city.

They heaved both of the bodies into the reeking pit and returned to deal with Jesus. Seeing Mary, his mother, and the other women, they more carefully lowered Jesus' cross and removed the nails from his body. Then they gently placed him in the arms of his mother, and stood back in silence while Mary and the others sobbed out their grief.

Joseph of Arimathea, a prestigious man in Jerusalem, had been a follower of Jesus but in secret because he feared the retaliation of the Jewish leaders. He now bravely displayed his allegiance by going to Pilatus and asking for the body. He returned with Nicodemus, a member of the Sanhedrin who had sincerely approached Jesus and was impressed by him. Joseph had a new tomb nearby, and Nicodemus provided a large quantity of burial spices. Both risked the displeasure of the chief priests because of what they were doing.

The centurion released the rest of the cohort except Clavicus. After giving Mary and the women a respectful time for mourning, he and Clavicus lifted Jesus' body and carried it to Joseph's tomb and placed it on the embalming table inside the door. When Clavicus came out of the tomb, he saw me standing there, and coming near to me, he whispered: "Thank you for forgiving me." "You are a fine man," I replied, "and I suspect you will find the kingdom of God in the near future. Now go in peace." With that, I embraced him. He was shocked at first and tensed up and tried to draw back, but after a moment he softened in my arms and hugged me back. When we separated, he looked into my eyes and said: "I wish I had had a father like you."

"I would have been proud to have you as a son," I responded. "My only child was a son, and he died at childbirth. I have longed for someone like you in my life." Not being used to such an emotional response, and obviously moved by my words, he nodded, touched my arm, and rejoined his centurion a short distance away.

Joseph and Nicodemus embalmed the body of Jesus with the spices and wrapped it in linen burial clothes, and then they summoned John the apostle and me to help them lift it onto the burial tablet. When all was completed, we exited the tomb, and the centurion and Clavicus rolled a large stone across the entrance.

Clavicus took the sign which he had removed from Jesus' cross and placed it on top of the stone. "Jesus of Nazareth," it read, "King of the Jews." Then the soldiers departed.

My eyes met those of Myriam, and there was a flash of connection and regard in the glance. Then John led the women away, and I was left there, outside the tomb, alone.

I sat there in my grief for a while, but then I realized that it was nearly dark, and that I shouldn't be on the streets this late on the eve of the Sabbath. It dawned on me that for the first time in over two years, I had nowhere to go for the night. My loneliness and aloneness really hit me, and I missed Jesus and the apostles terribly. I was really alone.

I started down the hill and passed a group of soldiers heading back up. One recognized me from earlier in the day and mentioned that they had been assigned to guard the tomb so Jesus' followers didn't steal the body and then claim that he had risen from the dead.

I decided to head for my old home, but Shadow had other ideas and led me along a different route. We finally reached the building where we had had the Passover meal just the night before. So much had happened in one day, I thought to myself. Shadow led me up the steps and I tried the door, but it was locked. I stood there, not knowing what to do, and then I decided to try the door again. When I rattled it, a challenging voice inside said "Who's there?" "David, the Elder," I replied, and I heard the locks on the door being opened. Once inside, I realized that the apostles and many of the women present at the crucifixion were now hiding there, and an aura of fear permeated the room.

Peter rushed to me and fell at my feet, wrapping his arms around my legs in anguish. "I have sinned greatly against our Master," he said, "and I disgraced myself in front of you and John. My first opportunity to be a witness for Jesus, but instead I betrayed him three times." Instead of immediately consoling him, I stood there for a long time and allowed him to sob out his pain. Then I sat down on the floor next to him and said: "We were all afraid, and none of us handled the situation in the best manner. Jesus knows we are all human, and I know that he has already forgiven us."

"But you and John stayed with him the whole time," Peter said in a pained voice, "while I ran like a scared animal." "That is true," I replied, "and now you have learned from your mistake and will be stronger in the future. The lesson for you is that our strength comes from Jesus and not from ourselves."

Mary was an inspiration to all of us, sitting quietly in her grief, calm and unafraid. The others were terrified, knowing that the religious leaders might find them and drag them all off to their deaths as well. I remembered that Jesus had told me that he would be counting on me to be a source of strength for the others, so I changed my demeanor and began to quietly pray in a composed manner. "Jesus promised us that this would end well," I said, "and he also said that we would see him again when he rises on the third day. Let's have faith in what he has told us." Hearing this, some of the apostles were openly skeptical, since they had never fully understood what Jesus meant when he talked about "rising from the dead." They could only think about a future of being hunted down and then persecuted by the religious leaders. No one among them could envision having the courage to come out in the open as followers of Jesus. It would be far too dangerous.

I rested and contemplated. At my age, I realized I had nothing to lose in this matter. I knew that I had already lived much longer than was expected, and that neither the religious leaders nor the Romans could take away my loyalty to Jesus. The apostles, however, were all younger, healthier men with a full life-time ahead of them, and I began to understand more fully why they would be terrified of the prospects awaiting them.

As I sat quietly, I made two stunning discoveries. First, I realized that my head had stopped hurting and that my wound was completely healed. Secondly, I realized that my clothes were clean, totally devoid of soiling or bloodstains despite what I had been through. I looked at Mary, and her robes were also spotless, despite having held the bloody, emaciated body of Jesus just a few hours before. It was indeed miraculous.

Phillip sat down next to me and shared the sad news that Judas had been found hung in a tree outside of the city walls, obviously despairing of ever being forgiven by Jesus. He also told me of some startling events at the time of Jesus' death. Not only had there been an earthquake, which I already knew, but the temple veil had been ripped asunder from top to bottom, and many long-since dead believers were seen alive by their families.

After a while, the apostles gathered around me and asked me to recount the events that had transpired since the arrest of Jesus outside the Garden of Olives. I described all of the painful details of Jesus' passion and death, beginning with his trial by the Sanhedrin.

The apostles were particularly moved when I disclosed the various things that Jesus had said while suffering, hung on the cross. They all recognized that Jesus demonstrated his holiness and compassion, even up to his death, and that he had died with dignity.

But the future looked bleak, and there was very little more that I could say except to encourage them to trust in Jesus, with whom they had been through so much together.

We stayed locked in the upper room, not knowing what else to do. There was a latrine on the lower level which we used as needed. The master of the house thankfully provided some food, because otherwise we would have gone without. None of us could go out and buy any, because Judas had held the purse of money and took it with him when he left.

Andrew brought me some goat's cheese, dried fish, and bread, and I realized I hadn't eaten in twenty-four hours nor had I slept very much either. After my much-appreciated meal and lots of water, I found a quiet corner and fell into a fitful, nightmare-filled sleep.

And so we remained during the Sabbath. Gloomy faces anticipated a bitter end for all of us, and I became frustrated by their pessimistic attitudes. "How many times did Jesus promise us that he would rise on the third day?" I asked in an exasperated tone, but none of them could comprehend the possibility of his reappearance, despite the fact that all of them had witnessed him raising several other people from the dead, including Lazarus. So I overcame my frustration and sat quietly, conversing with one or the other when they approached me, and doing what I did best, which was to listen caringly to their concerns.

CLAVICUS' CONVERSION

I saw Clavicus at a later date, and he recounted for me in vivid detail the events of the first day of the new week as he had experienced them. It seems that the Roman guard was changed every eight hours at the tomb, and he had been ordered to take up his sentry duty at midnight at the end of the Jewish Sabbath, along with three other soldiers. They spent the night snacking and making small-talk and taking turns sleeping.

At the first hint of dawn, when there was just enough light to begin to see, the stone sealing the tomb started to roll back of its own accord, and the startled gasps of the soldiers who were awake awoke those who were sleeping. A bright light appeared inside the tomb, and the other three soldiers became terrified and fled on foot down the hill.

Clavicus, however, was paralyzed in his place; he remained frozen to the ground, frightened but also curious as to what was about to transpire. The first thing he noticed was that as the stone was rotating away from the opening, the sign he had placed above it pronouncing Jesus' kingship remained on top of it as it rotated, rather than falling off.

Then a voice from inside said "Clavicus, Clavicus, see and believe." A figure appeared in the entrance of the tomb, and Jesus said to him, "Come and examine the wound from your spear, and believe that it is I who now lives again. Learn all that you can about me, for I will need you to testify on my behalf when you return to Rome. Jesus then showed him the spear wound, and Clavicus fell on his knees, saying "Truly, you are my only God. I now believe David was right. Bless this wonderful day."

REDEMPTION

Mary, the former sinner from Magdala whom Jesus had forgiven, went to the tomb to weep and mourn for her loss. This apparently was only shortly after Clavicus had left. She found the stone rolled away and the tomb empty. Two men dressed in bright white were inside the tomb. They told her that Jesus had risen and was no longer there. She went outside and saw a man standing there, whom she supposed to be a gardener. The man was in fact Jesus, and she finally recognized him when he uttered her name, "Mary," and she responded by saying "Teacher." She ran to the upper room to tell us the news, and Peter and John left our presence and quickly ran to the tomb to check out her story.

There they found the tomb empty, as she had reported, so they returned to tell us about it. When they came back, Peter was still unsure about what had happened, but John was convinced that Jesus had risen as he had promised, especially because the burial linen and head covering were neatly folded and set aside. Discussion broke out among the men, with arguments made both for and against Jesus' resurrection. Hope returned to most of our hearts, and we began singing prayers and blessing God for his goodness. Thomas volunteered to go out onto the streets to see if there was any word of Jesus' resurrection.

The apostles locked the doors after Thomas left, and so we were startled when we sensed a mysterious presence in the room. Jesus was suddenly manifested. "Peace be with you," he said; "do not be afraid, for it is I, risen as I promised. Peace be with you. I will be sending you out into the world to do my work. Do not be afraid." Then he was gone.

Other disciples joined us, reporting that they had seen Jesus on the road to Emmaus but did not recognize him at first. He had explained the meaning of his passion and death, using voluminous references to the prophecies of old, but they still didn't recognize him until he blessed and broke the bread at the evening meal and then disappeared.

When Thomas came back, he reported that there was no news on the street about Jesus being risen, so we told him all that had transpired, but he did not believe us, insisting that he needed flesh and blood proof before he would be convinced. For our part, we resumed singing songs of praise and thanksgiving, but we did not know what else we should be doing, and we kept the doors locked in fear of the wrath of the religious leaders.

Some time later, again despite the doors being locked, Jesus was manifested in the room, and after greeting us with "Shalom, peace be with you," he went directly to Thomas and said "Probe the nail marks with your finger, and put your hand into the spear wound in my side. Stop doubting and believe." Thomas responded "My Lord and my God."

This time Jesus tarried longer. Although he did not allow anyone to touch him, he went first to his mother and assured her of his love. Next he came to me and then to John, thanking us both for our faithfulness by being present during his suffering and death. He then spoke to the other apostles as well, and before leaving he commanded us to go to Galilee, where we would be reunited with him again. The next morning we unlocked the doors and bravely stepped out onto the street, on the way to Galilee to meet our Savior.

GALILEE

We proceeded through Judea and into Samaria, spreading the good news to everyone we met along the way. Some believed us, others did not, but all could see that we were empowered and jubilant about something. The apostles were eager to get home, but it took us several days to get there because they slowed their pace to accommodate my inability to walk fast. We sang and prayed along the way and wondered what the future held in store for us. We met many old friends, many of whom had been healed by Jesus.

When we reached Galilee we pressed on toward Capernaum, passing Nazareth and Magdala and traversing the rich and fertile Plains of Genneserat. Once in Capernaum, it was a grand reunion. Jesus had been very popular among the people there, to a point where he had even made the small town his home base during his ministry. Now we spread the great news among all the inhabitants, and most believed and praised God.

However, we did not find Jesus there, and after some anxious days, we began to wonder if we had clearly understood what he had told us to do. The men became restless and somewhat directionless, and one day, in the company of many of the apostles, Peter, always a man of action, announced that he was going fishing. A large number of his fellow apostles said that they would go with him, and I joined them as well. We fished all night and did not catch a single fish, but at least the activity was a diversion that kept us busy while we awaited enlightenment regarding what we were supposed to do next.

EMPOWERMENT

At dawn as we headed ashore, we saw a man standing at the water's edge. "Men," the figure said, "haven't you caught anything?" "Nothing," we answered. He instructed us to throw the net over the right side of the boat, and while we were tired and discouraged, we nevertheless did as he instructed. When we went to retrieve the net, we could not pull it back in because it was so filled with fish. "That man is the Lord," John shouted loudly.

Hearing this, Peter jumped into the water and began swimming toward shore, while the rest of us rowed the boat shoreward, dragging the net full of fish behind us. Once ashore, we saw that Jesus had built a fire and had some fish on it, and some bread off to one side.

"Bring some of the fish you just caught," he instructed, so Peter dragged in the net full of fish, cleaning several of them and adding them to those already on the fire. "Come and eat," the man said. The apostles guessed that it was Jesus, even though he had a very different, almost surreal appearance. After the meal, He spoke directly to Peter: "Do you love me?" he asked. "Yes, Lord" Peter responded, "I love you." "Take care of my lambs," Jesus replied. And a second time: "Peter, do you loved me?", and Peter responded "Yes, Lord, I love you." "Take care of my sheep." And yet a third time: "Peter, do you love me?" at which a saddened Peter responded: "Lord, you know everything; you know that I love you." And Jesus replied: "Take care of my sheep." By this,

Jesus reconfirmed that Peter was to be the apostle's leader. Later they appreciated the symbolism of Jesus asking him three times, to correspond to the three times that Peter had denied knowing him.

FAREWELL

Jesus spent time with us giving clear instructions on what we were supposed to do from that time forward. He said that he was going away, and when we expressed sorrow about this, he shared that it was necessary so that his Spirit could come and empower us. When he instructed us to return to Jerusalem, many of the apostles again became afraid because of the threat of retaliation on the part of the religious leaders. Jesus assured us that he would be with us at all times, and that he would return at a later point "to bring all men to him."

One day he took us up on a high hill, and suddenly he was visible only to me. Embracing me first, he said: "Go to Jerusalem and wait with the others in the upper room; your work is essentially done, but I want you to have the gift of my Spirit too. The morning after the Spirit descends, someone will be waiting for you at the East Gate with a cup of the best bravitzka ever brewed," he said with a smile. "Take her into your home. Use the precious gem you found and gave to me; it is still in your carry-bag. It is my wedding gift to you. Take it to Caleb, the bankrupt man with the crippled son. He has prospered and he will give you a fair price for it. Give half of the proceeds to the apostles, and use the other half to live on. Have a good life, and always know how much your strength, wisdom, loyalty and love have meant to me. Your presence under the cross helped me immensely. I love you, David." He broke our embrace, and then, starting with Peter, Jesus spoke with the rest of the apostles, one at a time. After the last apostle, Jesus raised his hand and blessed us all, promising to be with us always, and then he disappeared into the sky.

THE FIRE OF CONVICTION

We retraced our steps to Jerusalem, growing more apprehensive as we approached the city. We decided to again hide in the upper room, and we gathered enough provisions in advance so that we could keep the door locked and not have to go out into the streets.

We waited for many days, singing and praying, but this time, instead of despair and anxiety, we were filled with hope and expectation. One day, our prayer was interrupted by the sounds of a strong wind, and despite the fact that all of the doors and windows were closed, the wind appeared to be blowing through the room where we were staying.

Small flames appeared above each of our heads, and I felt a warmth spread through my body like that produced by a cup of strong wine. An exuberance coursed through me that bordered on ecstasy; I felt joy and power and thankfulness to God, all at the same time.

The others felt the same way. We threw open the doors and spilled out into the street, singing and praising God. A crowd had already assembled, because the strong wind had been audible throughout the neighborhood. I heard the apostles talking in foreign tongues. I spotted Clavicus, who was guarding that sector of the city that day. He ran to me, saying: "I saw him, I saw him alive, I saw the spear wound, I believe, he is now my only God." I hugged him warmly, and he returned my embrace. To my surprise, I began speaking in Latin: "Come see me when you are off duty," I said, "and we'll talk more about all that has transpired!"

MYRIAM

I didn't sleep at all that night, and the next morning, long before sunrise, I hurried to the East Gate. A figure emerged from the shadows, and this time I wasn't afraid. It was Myriam, holding a basket containing cups of hot bravitzka and warm pastries. We sat down on a nearby stone wall. I was tongue-tied, and hardly knew what to say. She had aged considerably, but she was still beautiful to me. I looked at her for a long time.

Finally she smiled and said: "The answer is 'Yes,' David." "But I haven't even said anything yet," I responded, "although my heart is full of things I want to say. I just can't seem to get them out." She smiled. "I've waited this long, but I'm not going to wait any longer," she said teasingly. "You'd better quickly find a way to tell me what you want me to know." "I've cared for you since the night Jesus was born," I began. "I admired your thoughtfulness and skill, and your seeing everything that needed to be done, and your doing everything at once, and especially your humility in not seeking any thanks."

"My heart leapt when I saw you at the temple when Jesus was presented, and I've missed you and thought of you and loved you ever since. I've been starved for you, and I have not known full happiness without you. I want you to spend the rest of your life with me." "Is that a proposal of marriage?" she said, teasing me again. "Yes," I asserted,

"come be my wife. I'm not going to wait any longer, either."
"The answer is still 'Yes'," she said, and we finally held each
other in a warm embrace after so many years of painful
longing.

EPILOGUE

Myriam and David were married in the temple, with Mary of Magdala and Andrew the Apostle serving as witnesses. The couple took up residence in David's home, and to his delight, his coins were still hidden there and his tools still safely secreted in his neighbor's hiding place. He was expected to retire, but instead he again took up his leather-working trade.

More importantly, he reclaimed his seat in the Sanhedrin and became a vocal supporter of the apostles and their followers. His outspokenness was a thorn in the leaders' sides, but since they had no legal grounds to expel him, they instead began plotting to kill him with poison, making it appear like a natural death. A Jew who spied for the Romans got wind of the plot and reported it to the Roman centurion, who in turn took the information to Pilatus. Pilatus summoned the chief priests to the Antonium and warned them sternly that he would deal harshly with them if David was ever harmed.

David became highly respected by members of the Sanhedrin, some of whom approached him with sincere questions about Jesus. Younger members came to his home, and he spent hours showing them how Jesus had fulfilled the prophecies of old. In this way, David was passing on the gift given to him by Zechariah previously. Apostles, disciples and other followers of Jesus also visited his home and profited from his wisdom and counsel. He was a man of prayer and also the elderly mentor everyone respected and admired.

The young, new movement began to flourish, despite the opposition of the chief priests. The movement was especially characterized by the concern of its members for the poor, widows, orphans, and others in need.

Peter and the other apostles shrugged off imprisonment and beatings, and continued to ignore the warnings of the religious leaders by preaching the gospel in public. David received a sizable amount of money from Caleb as payment for the precious gem he had found; he gave half the money to the apostles as Jesus had directed, and it was used to benefit the beggars of the city, the poor and the homeless.

Joshua was made one of the first deacons of the new group and devoted the rest of his life to ministering to the beggars of the city, bringing them not only food and clothing but also his irresistible joy and the good news of salvation.

Bartinaeus, the blind beggar who was given his sight by Jesus, was true to his word and became a permanent member of the new movement and a loving servant to the blind, sitting with sightless beggars for long hours while he shared the good news of permanent light and peace in eternity. Some were healed of their blindness through his ministry, while others, while remaining blind, were nevertheless led to believe in the good news of salvation.

The new religion spread rapidly. Countless numbers of Jews had encountered Jesus personally and were impressed by him, and so many had seen him after he rose from the dead that the fact of his resurrection was incontrovertible. The apostles spread out into the entirety of the known world, and one by one, they eventually were martyred for their faith, all except John, that is, who fled the persecution by taking Jesus' mother to Greece.

Clavicus returned to Rome, and while still a legionnaire, became an ardent promoter of the gospel, supporting Paul and his work after Paul was imprisoned in Rome. Clavicus was one of the first martyrs of the new movement; refusing to obey an officer's order to kill a Christian, he was subsequently crucified himself by his fellow soldiers.

Myriam and David lived a full and healthy life for many more years, and after David died a painless death with a large number of apostles and other believers praying at his bedside. Myriam died peacefully in her sleep shortly thereafter, and was undoubtedly united with her beloved David and also with Jesus in heaven forever.

18542109R00177

Made in the USA
Charleston, SC
09 April 2013